"With compassion, clarity, and a beautiful collaborative spirit, Drs. Helsel and Harris-Smith give parents and caregivers a powerful gift. Answering real questions we might be afraid to ask, providing concrete tools to help us know and *do* better—ourselves and with our kids, *The ABCs of Diversity* equips us to be co-conspirators in creating a justice- and love-infused future of flourishing for all. Read this book." —Jennifer Harvey, author of *Raising White Kids: Bringing Up Children in a Racially Unjust America*

"If every parent of every child reads this book, this next generation will truly create the kind of world we all want to live in—where radical difference is something to be celebrated, where every human being enjoys peace and safety, and where our own hearts are not ruled by fear and hatred." —Kerry Connelly, author of *Good White Racist? Confronting Your Role in Racial Injustice*

"Building a beloved community of acceptance and belonging begins with our children. *The ABCs of Diversity* provides us with building blocks to engage young (and not so young) hands and hearts in constructing a way of being a more just and equitable society. A countercultural way to put flesh on the *imago dei.*" —Leah Gunning Francis, vice president for academic affairs at Christian Theological Seminary and the author of *Ferguson and Faith: Sparking Leadership and Awakening Community*

"Covering topics from 'the talk,' gender, identify formation, and talking to children and adolescents about difference, *The ABCs of Diversity* provides readers strategies, practices, and accessible entry points into the life-affirming, and for some of us life-saving, conversations that are necessary in today's world. Helsel and Harris-Smith provide a tool kit for any parent, small group leader, or individual looking to build deeper relationships across differences." —Patrick Reyes, author of *Nobody Cries When We Die: God, Community, and Surviving to Adulthood*

THE
ABCs
OF
DIVERSITY

Helping Kids (and Ourselves!)
Embrace Our Differences

CAROLYN B. HELSEL & Y. JOY HARRIS-SMITH

chalice
press

Saint Louis, Missouri

An imprint of Christian Board of Publication

Cover design: Jennifer Pavlovitz

ChalicePress.com

Print: 9780827200937
EPUB: 9780827200944
EPDF: 9780827200951

Printed in the United States of America

Dedication

Carolyn: For Phil, Caleb, and Evelyn, who teach me
kindness and wonder everyday.
Y. Joy: For Leon, Asa, and Eden, my beacons of light on
this journey called life.

* * * * *

*This book is made possible, in part,
due to a generous gift from Darryl and Shari Searuggs
in honor of Emmitt Searuggs Jr. and in loving memory of
Eddie Holliness, their beloved fathers. Born and raised in
the segregated south, Emmitt and Eddie fully embraced
everyone's humanity regardless of race, ethnicity,
or cultural background.*

* * * * *

Contents

Preface

This book will help you learn the language of difference and diversity. In it, we break down the complex concepts and ideas from the most recent scholarship on multicultural education, intercultural communication, and diversity and inclusion studies to help you use these concepts in your own life. We assume you are a busy person, without the time to read thousands of pages of books on these subjects. We, on the other hand, have the privilege of reading books for a living, and we want to share the knowledge we have gained over time through these books and through practice.

We are also both mothers, trying to teach our children the language of difference. Joy has two preschool-aged children, and Carolyn has an elementary-aged student and a middle-schooler. Carolyn is white and lives in Austin, Texas. Joy is black and lives in New York City.

Both of us teach for a living. We teach adults, so this book is written with adults in mind. Joy has taught junior high and high school in NYC public school, and Carolyn has volunteered as a Girl Scout troop leader, basketball coach, and Sunday School teacher, so both of us also know how to talk to children. Understanding the processes of learning has helped us come up with ways we hope will facilitate your learning—such as using acronyms to help you remember some of the core ideas, practical tips and advice for things you can say to your children and to others, and lists of additional resources to which you can turn if you want to learn more on a particular topic.

The book's strategy is threefold:

First, it offers information about the different kinds of diversity that we are already experiencing in our communities. Knowledge is one of the first ways we can begin building better tools for communicating with one another and growing in our ability to relate to others. This book deals with issues of *race and ethnicity, gender, sexuality, religion and politics, nationality, and culture.* There are many other forms of diversity that we could have included here, such as economics, learning styles, physical and mental abilities/ disabilities, and language, but we have had to limit ourselves. Nonetheless, you will likely find some of the concepts and ideas presented to be helpful for thinking and talking about other kinds of difference.

Second, we offer our own stories as parents and teachers trying to learn more about the diverse world in which we are living, and we share our own experiences of trying to navigate this diverse world in the classroom and with our own children. We share out of a belief that we are all still learning and growing, and that many adults, like children, still need to learn the basics of how to communicate with persons who are different from themselves. While this is primarily a book to help you with raising your own children or teaching in a diverse setting, it is also a book to help you navigate this diverse world yourself.

Third, our focus is on being practical. So we include appendices of activities, books, and curriculum suggestions that you can use to talk with children at various ages and stages, as well as in discussions with other adults. For persons who are tired of the theoretical platitudes and big ideas that have no purchase in everyday reality, we offer you real tools to use: activities that help you foster conversations with young children or youth, scripts you can practice to help you respond when kids say things that reveal they are noticing the differences around them, and suggestions of books that can help kids learn by reading about people different from themselves.

We also realize that you are already doing amazing things in the world to advocate for diversity, and so we hope to hear from you. We hope this book will spark your imagination for community work that you can instigate to help bring about greater understanding among the people all around you. Perhaps you will be inspired to run storytelling events or communal get-togethers that invite shared hospitality and vulnerability. Perhaps you will want to offer workshops or book groups to other parents in your neighborhood to develop greater compassion and understanding. Tell us what you do! If you are a teacher, you probably have a lot of advice you can share with us regarding what you are already doing and saying in your classroom to help your students foster a more welcoming and inclusive environment for all learners. You can share your ideas with us and other readers at our website, abcsofdiversity.com.

To live together in the world house that we are building, we need to understand the foundations that will help sustain a healthy community. We hope this book gives you a theoretical framework for understanding our differences so that you can think through other major decisions and potential conflicts that may not be covered explicitly in this book. We also hope to encourage you on the journey by helping you understand your own emotions and processes about diversity, so that you are more likely to stay engaged for the long haul.

With those primary goals in mind, you will see that the chapters are laid out thematically. In the Introduction, we share with you some of our personal goals and trepidations around this book, naming our assumptions and hopes for what you might get out of it.

Chapter 1 provides the context for this book: what we mean by the ABCs of diversity and how those letters can be an acronym for helping us be mindful of our own responses. There are three incrementally more involved ways that we conceive of the ABCs of diversity:

#1. *Afraid, Back away,* and *Control*: our automatic ABCs

#2. *Acknowledge, Be present,* and *Come closer*: the ABCs of intentional engagement

#3. *Access, Build,* and *Cultivate*: the ABCs of a more just society

Chapter 2 looks at the earliest forms of identity that children begin to inhabit: race and gender. This chapter unpacks some of the meanings of "identity" and how that word can be both something we assign to others and something we claim for ourselves. In addition, this chapter explores the ramifications of identity on both marginalized and privileged persons. Identity, whether by choice or assigned, affects us all.

Chapter 3 looks at the multiracial world in which we live and the statistics around growing diversity in the United States. Thinking about the world our children are entering, even before they are born, heightens our awareness of what is happening in the society they will inherit. We are going through a painful growth spurt as a nation, and we need to understand why that is and how we can respond to mitigate the pain.

Chapter 4 takes a deeper dive into the ideas of gender and sexuality. It looks at current research behind the variety of ways in which people experience themselves as male or female, or as non-binary, and how our gender identity is not the same as our sexual orientation.

Chapter 5 looks at the importance of naming racial difference as a means to help kids develop positive ways to view themselves in a society that still racializes people into categories, whether or not we accept those categories.

Chapter 6 focuses on religious diversity and the ways that we can learn from one another by sharing our values and our deeply held commitments to care for one another.

Chapter 7 both affirms and challenges the ways we use social media, and how it can be used to drive us further apart. As with each of these chapters, we show how to engage differences by returning to the chapter 1 ABCs about intentionally cultivating relationships with persons different from yourself and building communities of diversity both online and in person.

Finally, chapter 8 looks at how even as adults we need to be learning and growing, since without such growth we still tend to hurt one another with our comments and attitudes. We all operate with some kind of a code of ethics or moral philosophy. This chapter asks you to go deeper and reflect critically about what you say you believe and what you actually do, inviting you to consider, "How well does what I say and what I do line up?"

Through further reading and curriculum suggestions, in the appendices we offer concrete suggestions for how parents can help their own children and the children for whom they care. We hope these resources will help you bring to life the ideas of the book. Perhaps you will find yourself engaging your own family members or friends or community, helping others to better understand these categories of diversity. These activities and curriculum suggestions are just a start. No doubt you have others, and we hope you will share some of them on our website, abcsofdiversity.com.

Thanks for joining us. We are glad to be on this journey with you!

Introduction

Do you have any doubts or insecurities when it comes to talking about issues of "diversity"? Are you unsure what the word even means? Are you afraid of the conflict that might underlie diversity? Do you consciously or subconsciously walk away from the subject or situations of diversity because you avoid stirring things up, or do you prefer to stick to situations and areas of discussion in which you feel more comfortable?

Yes? Then you're in good company. We are Carolyn Helsel and Y. Joy Harris-Smith, and we are both moms and professors. Joy's kids are currently preschoolers, and Carolyn's kids are in elementary and middle school, and we both teach adults of all ages who are interested in working in non-profits or churches. Carolyn is white, and though she has written books on talking about racism with white people, talking about issues of diversity *still* makes her feel insecure and a bit nervous. Joy, on the other hand, *lives* diversity everyday as a black woman, married to a man from a culture different from the one in which she grew up. With experience teaching in the New York City school system and doctoral work in communication and culture, Joy knows well the challenges inherent in these kinds of conversations.

So why are we writing a book about issues of diversity and race, especially when these conversations cause us angst? For one simple reason: love.

Love makes us write. As moms, we love our kids. Getting to interact with our kids and their friends through after-school activities, we begin to love their friends. Teaching adults from different walks of life in our jobs, we come across those who have different opinions about issues of sexuality and politics. We fall in love with them as well (ok, not every single one, but even those hard-to-love students are still teaching us in some ways, and we are grateful for that).

And love makes us notice things. We notice white children on the playground being rude to children of color, and parents remaining silent. We notice youth being teased for being different. We notice young adults struggling with their identity as gay or lesbian or bisexual—especially in the context of religion, since many of them come from backgrounds where religious leaders have taught them that who they love makes them an abomination. We notice straight people who come from religious communities where people still believe that being gay will send you to hell, who are themselves struggling to reconcile these deeply held religious beliefs with their own relationships with friends and co-workers who are gay.

Are you feeling uncomfortable yet? We are too. We do not want to offend anyone. We worry about what you, the reader, are thinking right now. We are afraid you will put this book down, assuming this book is not speaking to you because it is too liberal, or too conservative.

See? Already we have put each other into boxes. "Liberal." "Conservative." And we walk away. If we don't want to talk to someone who doesn't think like us or vote like us, then we don't have to. We can cloister ourselves with like-minded folk and stay on our separate sides.

But we do not want to live like this.

And we have a feeling that you don't either.

You may work with people who have different opinions about politics, or who come from different cultural backgrounds or ethnicities. Perhaps you work with people from around the world. You may have someone in your own family who has a different take on things than you do, and you love this person even though you have differences.

Our kids are growing up in a world of greater diversity than ever before. They may know kids who have two moms or two dads, come from seven different countries, and speak four different languages.

Friends of our children may have different religions they celebrate, or no religious background whatsoever.

Kids may not learn the language of race in their classroom curriculum, but soon enough news and media about racism and "white people" and "black people" and "Latinx" filter into their world, and our kids may or may not see how these terms relate to them, if at all.

Kids who have a mom from Nigeria and a dad from France may grow up knowing two different cultures by visiting their parents' home countries, identify as much with their French relatives as their Nigerian family, and be baffled why others view them simply as "black" in America.

Children of Korean American parents who have been in the United States for several generations may not understand why people say they are "Asian," when they have never stepped foot on the Asian continent.

You may have a child in your family or in your kid's school whom everyone calls "David," but who in preschool was known as "Tessa."

But what if this all sounds like too much political correctness, like there is pressure on us to check all the boxes and say all the right things? What if these differences make us more than a little nervous ourselves, since we may never have interacted with people from backgrounds that our kids are getting to know?

It does not feel good to know less than our kids do, and as they get older, they remind us just how much we do not know.

But if they are already learning about all of this by interacting with their peers, then why should we grown-ups have to learn about it, too? Can't we just leave it to our kids to sort out our differences? They already seem to be a lot more accepting of different kinds of people than we and our parents are.

If you have any of these impulses, you are not alone. We feel them too. We want to believe our kids are smart enough and kind enough to learn how to build a better society than the one in which we are living now. We want to trust that their future is going to have greater peace and understanding than the world they inhabit today. And not knowing enough about people who are different from us makes us afraid of getting it wrong. Of passing along stereotypes. Of offending someone.

So we avoid talking about differences altogether.

But that feels a lot like abdicating our responsibility as parents to teach our children how to be good citizens and how to contribute positively to society.

We want our kids to live long, healthy, and happy lives, and for us that means that they are able to be in good relationships with persons from different backgrounds whose different life experiences can greatly enhance our own kids' knowledge and understanding of the world. We want them to be kind and to learn to live with people who are different from themselves, because that is our world now, and we want them to thrive in it.

We think you want the same for your kids, too.

Dear reader, at any point that you feel challenged or uncomfortable by the words that are expressed here—don't quit. Pause, take a break, go for a walk, or just close your eyes and breathe—but come back. Please. You are making good progress. Keep going! We are all in this together.

—Carolyn and Joy

The ABCs of Diversity

The Reverend Doctor Martin Luther King Jr. wrote in 1967 that we are living in a world house with all of humanity and that in order to sustain our civilization we need to be able to work together and support one another. King wrote:

> Our hope for creative living in this world house that we have inherited lies in our ability to reestablish the moral ends of our lives in personal character and social justice. Without this spiritual and moral reawakening we shall destroy ourselves in the misuse of our own instruments.[1]

Learning how to live with one another on this planet is more than a matter of political correctness or naïve optimism: it is a matter of humanity's survival. We need a spiritual and moral reawakening in order to live peacefully together in this world house. We also need to be willing to roll up our sleeves and help build or restore this world house.

So what does it take to build community? How do we communicate across the enormous cultural divides that are a part of every nation, race, region, religion, community, and family? How do we relate to the many different cultures with which we come into contact on a daily basis?

---

[1]Martin Luther King Jr., *Where Do We Go from Here: Chaos or Community?* (1967; reprint, Boston: Beacon Press, 2010), 183.

The Language of Difference

To help our children and to live as better citizens in our diverse society, we need to learn a new language. The "language of diversity" is not strictly a spoken language, such as English or Spanish, but rather an awareness of the challenges present today and a fluency in being able to talk with people who have different opinions than us on important issues. The language of diversity is not about facts of cultural etiquette or food and festivals from people and cultures around the world, but rather about the mindset it takes to engage in relationships with others.

Learning to embrace the differences all around us requires knowing how to speak this language. When you are with someone who is different from you, you are learning a new kind of language—even if you both speak English. When talking across our differences—whether difference of gender, race or ethnicity, sexual orientation, nationality, ability, or simply talking to a family member in the Northeast when you have been raised in the South— we are talking through cultural filters and assumptions that shape the way we speak to and with one another.

This sounds complicated, and it is. But just as infants learn the highly complicated language of their parents through being around them, so too you have picked up how to speak to others based on cultural messages. It is both a conscious and a subconscious skill. You are constantly "reading" other people and figuring out what's the appropriate way to communicate.

What happens when we are proficient in one language and we come across someone speaking a different one? We get confused, and we may feel a little lost. When we are in spaces where there are a lot of cultural differences, it may feel as if others are speaking an unfamiliar language, and we may feel uncertain and wonder, What's the right thing to say?

All of us learn by doing and making mistakes along the way. We watch children develop and try out words and phrases they hear from other members of the family. Through the media, we pick up on new uses of language and learn new words to describe our own experiences. Language itself is constantly evolving and changing, and youth are among the first to pick up new forms of slang until it becomes standard.

If language is so easy to absorb, then why do we need to learn it? We learn language in school to communicate better with a wider audience. The more adept we are at a language, the greater our capacity to speak, write, and read it—and chances are we will be able to communicate more effectively. Language learning is both simple and complex, challenging and rewarding. We learn to speak a language by conversing with others.

The language of diversity is similar to the language we learn at home and at school. Language is dynamic. It is constantly evolving; new words and ideas come into use to help us better describe our experiences. And language is something we need to continue to learn. Some ideas and the words that go with them we typically learn through additional education—they're ones we would not just pick up on our own.

When we learn to speak the language of diversity, we are better able to communicate with a wider array of others. When we learn to "read" the language of diversity, we can more easily understand complex human interactions at home, at work, and in society. When we learn to use the language of diversity with our children, then they, too, can be better citizens in our increasingly diverse society.

How do we learn this language of diversity? Just like we learn other kinds of languages. In addition to learning through practice, we learn through picking apart the language into its smallest parts— the language's alphabet. Teachers introduce language to children through the alphabet and by helping children make connections between the letters they see and the sounds they hear. A visual aid to a child's learning might include a poster with a single letter, with pictures of some of the words that begin with that letter. In addition to having a visual representation of the letter "A," for instance, a child sees a picture of apples. On a poster with the letter "B," a child might see a picture of a banana, and so forth. Children learn letters by connecting the concept of a single letter to another concept, like a food they know by name. They know the sound of the name of the food or other object, and this helps them remember the sound that the letter makes.

In learning the language of diversity, we authors want to try and break down into smaller components the larger ideas surrounding intercultural communication. We also want to show you how you can help your children learn this language alongside you, because just like you, they need to learn the language of difference.

Since our children are growing up amidst greater cultural diversity than previous generations, won't they inherently or automatically know this language of difference? No. Why? Because of shifts in language and culture. Just as there have been shifts in language and its use, so too there have been shifts in the world and across cultures. So we can't assume that our children can figure out such things on their own.

Children do not automatically learn the language of difference. They absorb the same cultural biases and messages the rest of us receive, and those biases and cultural filters prevent them from being able to engage thoughtfully with persons who are different from them. They may learn language about what is "for boys" or "for girls," but this does not help them to speak about how girls and boys can be very different from those stereotypes or norms. They need adults who can help them speak a new language, one that does not rely on old scripts to tell them what distinguishes boys from girls, persons of different religions, people from different races or ethnicities, and other differences they will encounter. We all need to learn this language, and because the language continually changes and evolves, we need to keep on learning.

To assist you in learning the language of difference, we have come up with three ways of conceptualizing some of its basic building blocks. One of the ways we want to help you learn the language of difference is to be able to read your own language. So the first set of ABCs focuses on some of the predictable patterns that may prevent us from engaging with people and ideas that are different or unfamiliar. The second set of ABCs looks at how we can change our individual responses. The third set looks at the issue of diversity more broadly and how each of us can engage this language on a systemic level. These three ABCs build on one another, helping us to notice in which patterns we are already engaging, moving toward a commitment to engage with difference, and then following through with a larger-scale discussion of how each of us can make our diverse society work for everyone. We hope these frameworks can help you discover what gift you have to bring.

#1 Our Automatic ABCs: Afraid, Back away, Control

What are the messages you already are communicating about difference? What are the physical ways you respond to bodies that are different from your own? What are your emotional or affective responses when you encounter diversity day to day?

There may be many ways that you respond, and how you respond will depend upon the kind of difference you encounter. Next time you are in a place in which you are surrounded by people who are different from you—maybe it is a group of people with ethnic or racial difference, maybe it is a room full of people from a different political party—observe how you react. What goes on in your body? When we are in unfamiliar settings, or when we encounter differences that make us uncomfortable, we tend to respond in ways that make it harder for us to learn.

These predictable patterns of unhelpful responses can be remembered with the acronym ABC: we may feel *Afraid,* we may physically *Back away,* and we may have the impulse to *Control* the situation in some way. Afraid, Back away, Control: Do you recognize these reactions in yourself?

Being *afraid* of difference is a common feeling. We fear the unfamiliar, afraid of saying the wrong thing, making a mistake, being rejected. If we have been part of conversations about diversity and difference in the past and that have not gone well, we may be afraid of repeating a negative experience. We might fear hurting another person's feelings.

But fear might only be a momentary reaction. It may not even register consciously on our emotional radar. But look at your body language. What is your body saying in this moment? We're guessing you observe yourself *backing away.* If you are in a room with persons who are different from you, we imagine you stepping back from the group or staying on the periphery. Maybe you avoid making eye contact. A more extreme example is removing yourself from the space altogether. Perhaps your response is a verbal rather than physical one. Perhaps you back away from conversation by avoiding making conversation altogether. Backing away can include the ways we try to avoid diversity altogether, by staying in groups of like-minded people or by sticking with people we perceive as being like us.

Third, we all tend to react out of a desire to *control* the situation. Observe yourself as you respond to experiences with different people. Do you try to expose yourself to differences regularly? Or do you control your environment by making sure you are surrounded only by people with whom you share things in common?

Control as a response to difference can be seen societally as well, by looking at how at different points in history our society has responded to diversity. When we see whole neighborhoods segregated by race or class, this is control at a governmental and local level to maintain similarity among neighborhood residents. Such control usually takes the form of discrimination. Looking at the history of race in the United States, we can see how certain ethnic groups and people of color were forced to live in parts of the city that were separate from those where wealthier whites lived.

But even without these more blatant forms of discrimination, our need for control comes out in smaller ways: with whom we choose to sit, to whom we say hello, which person becomes our friend and which one remains an acquaintance. Control can be a subtle way in which we isolate ourselves from people who are different from us.

So if these three tendencies—being *Afraid, Backing away,* and *Control*—are *un*helpful responses to learning the language of diversity, how can we train ourselves to react differently and be more effective in our communication, responding with a greater sense of compassion and inclusivity toward others?

#2 *The ABCs of Intentional Engagement: Acknowledge, Be Present, Come Closer*

We suggest a second ABC: *Acknowledge, Be present,* and *Come closer.* These three responses can help you stay engaged in the process of learning more about diversity and can help you model embracing differences for your children.

Acknowledging, Being present, and *Coming closer* together form the initial steps we can all take toward greater intercultural understanding.

To *acknowledge* means that our first reaction should be to recognize the presence of diversity. When we start to feel uncomfortable, we can acknowledge the source of our discomfort. We can say to ourselves, "I am learning the language of difference. I am learning something new. I am not familiar with this setting or with persons from this particular background, and I am learning how to be in relationship with them." Acknowledge that there is something new happening in you and around you, and that this opportunity can be a gift. Acknowledge that this is hard for you, that you may make a mistake, and that you are somewhat afraid of the situation. Acknowledge that you have a reason to be learning the language of difference: to become more connected to the human family and to grow in community with others. Acknowledge that you are setting an example for your own children in learning this language for yourself.

To *be present* also means to be curious, to be open, to be willing to try and make mistakes. Being present means that you have acknowledged the opportunity to learn something new and you are being present or available and open to that opportunity. Having acknowledged the challenges you may have in learning about people different from yourself, you are able to be present to those feelings of discomfort. You are also able to turn that discomfort into curiosity. Be curious, and ask yourself, What can I learn from this experience? What are the messages I am receiving from this other person? Being present also means being willing to make mistakes, recognizing when you may be misreading the situation. You can ask yourself, In what ways might I be misunderstanding this person?

Third, a better response to learn the language of diversity is to *come closer*. Coming closer means physically remaining in spaces in which you are uncomfortable. Coming closer means actually moving closer toward persons who are different from you, rather than staying away or avoiding them. Choose to sit next to someone you do not know. Make eye contact and say hello to a stranger. In coming closer, you open yourself to learning about others through proximity. It means you extend the olive branch. It means that you *be* the change you wish to see in the world. It means you become a bridge without expectation. It means you initiate action. You can learn a language from a distance, but you cannot speak a language fluently unless you begin speaking with other people in that language.

Acknowledging difference, *Being present* to the diversity around you, and *Coming closer* to persons who are not like you are three ways you can begin to learn the language of difference. If you want to help yourself become a better communicator, to have deeper relationships with persons around you, and to be more effective as a citizen in a diverse society, you will benefit from starting with these ABCs. And if you want to help your own children grow up as compassionate and kind people, able to overcome their own discomfort in new situations, then you need to be able to model this for them in your own behavior.

#3 The ABCs of a More Just Society: Access, Build, Cultivate

So far, our ABCs have focused only on the inward experience of diversity, your own individual reaction to people who are different from you. But given the history of discrimination in this country, it is important that we also move towards interpersonal engagement and look at a broader perspective for addressing diversity. For instance, given the policies and practices that keep people of color in disadvantaged contexts, simply treating individual people better does not address the systemic challenges—the problems that pervade our systems, our institutions, our laws, our community practices. To do this, we need another set of ABCs.

Enter *Access, Build,* and *Cultivate* (ABC)!

Access refers to your ability to connect to knowledge, resources, and people. Accessing knowledge refers to your responsibility to learn more on your own. It refers to using information that you can find in libraries, studying the history of policies and institutions in your community, and engaging in workshops and professional developments that address diversity.

Access also refers to being the one to provide entry into a place or space that another person might not otherwise be able to enter. This is what is meant by accessing "resources." Each person has their own area of privilege and influence, and accessing resources means using what we have to benefit someone else, enabling them the same access we ourselves have. By providing access, you are also being an ally.

Access also means initiating an interaction between persons in your network and connections to which others may not have access. It means taking the initiative to be a bridge, rather than expecting someone else to be the bridge.

Build refers to the development of networks and frameworks based upon what has been accessed. It means not only allowing others access, but following through to see the establishment of those relationships. Building means being aware that society as we know it has already been *built* to be the way it is now, and that if we want our social structures to change, we need to build new forms of social connections. This way, the learning we do about diversity is not just learning for learning's sake, but to use that learning to build something for others, particularly structures from which those who are marginalized can finally also benefit.

Cultivate refers to generating something new with what has been accessed and built upon. Cultivate also refers to the fact that although processes and methods developed at one time may have worked at that time, cultivating something new recognizes that we need new methods and processes as we move into the future.

Cultivate is also a gardening word. It's knowing that you can eat the beet greens as well as the beet root. It's knowing how to put your garden bed to sleep—covering it with mulch, allowing the soil to rest—and then, when you're ready to plant again, knowing how to dig up the soil and plant or sow something new.

To cultivate is a life work—a work about tending to life, helping it flourish, and recognizing our own needs for nourishment along the way. Such work, such cultivation, requires critical self-reflection, digging deep within ourselves to find out what our beliefs are about ourselves and about others. It requires not just assuming that our work in accessing and building has made us immune from making mistakes, but being willing to cultivate a spirit of humility open to ongoing learning. It requires cultivating a healthy respect for the flourishing of all life and seeing how our own thriving is necessarily connected to the thriving of all living beings.

As you think about ways to teach and engage difference, remember to *Access, Build*, and *Cultivate*. Access the information and the people near you; build upon what you have accessed; and don't forget to cultivate the new relationships, networks, and opportunities to nourish life all around you, particularly those whose lives are the most threatened. When you access, build, and cultivate, there is always a refreshing that happens. The conversations do not get old and stale.

Summary Table of the ABCs

Notice the ABCs that you may be experiencing as you read this book.

#1: Automatic ABCs *(Unhelpful but Predictable Responses)*

A—Afraid	If you are *afraid*, ask yourself what makes you feel afraid in this space?
B—Back away	If you notice yourself physically wanting to *back away,* figure out why.

C—Control	If you notice the impulse in yourself to control the circumstances, figure out why. Observe your reactions. Write them down, rather than running away from them.

#2: Intentional ABCs (Personal Introspection to Stay Engaged)

A—Acknowledge	What happens when you *acknowledge* the diversity around you?
B—Be present	Notice how you can sit with the feeling of being uncomfortable, and *be present* to this opportunity.
C—Come closer	In what way could you physically *come closer* to someone and begin a conversation?

#3: Interpersonal ABCs (Building a More Just Society)

A—Access	What information do you have at your disposal for the interpersonal or social dynamics going on around you? To what resources (networks of relationships or skills) can you give others *access* to help them better navigate this situation?
B—Build	How can you *build* upon what you already know—or the resources you can access or the people you know—to build a deeper connection with others in this space?
C—Cultivate	What can you contribute to the mutual flourishing of yourself and the people you are getting to know? How can you *cultivate* within yourself a capacity for lifelong learning and adjusting to the new?

Chapter 1 Activity for Self-Reflection

Who Are the People in Your Neighborhood?

What are the places (religious institutions, neighborhoods, restaurants, shops) to which you can go to experience people who are different from you? It can be intimidating to go to a place where you are the only person who looks like you or sounds like you or believes the way you do.   However, go and try it.   Sit in a space where there is a language you do not understand, for example. Walk through the ABCs above, noting your own automatic responses as well as what your intentional or interpersonal responses might entail. Write about the experience and then share it in a group or class or with those who are interested in developing better relationships with others.

Identities We're Assigned at Birth

Before Birth: The Gender Reveal

When a woman is pregnant, other than "When's the due date?" people ask, "Do you know if it's a girl or a boy?"

Some parents choose to wait until the birth to find out their child's gender. Yet more and more, through ultrasound imaging, parents are finding out the gender of their baby-to-be before the child is born. Some even host "reveal parties" at which the gender of the baby is disclosed in some visual way in the presence of friends and family. These gender reveal parties can take a number of different forms, with videos of the reveal often being posted on the Internet for others to see. A friend of mine had someone insert colored powder into a golf ball and a tennis ball that, when hit, exploded with blue power, revealing their baby's gender to everyone in attendance: it's a boy! Other couples find out by asking their doctor to give the ultrasound results to a baker, who bakes a cake with pink or blue filling. And so on. A gender reveal party is a fun way to gather people together before a baby is born without the pressure of bringing gifts that come with a typical "baby shower."

But what do gender reveal parties reveal about us as a society? They tell us that before a baby is out of the womb, a gender identity has already been assigned by our society. We put great meaning on this gender identification, and it creates a lot of expectations for who this child will be. If it's a boy, we have a variety of assumptions: he will like the color blue; he will like playing with trucks and balls; he will be into sports, or at least play more aggressively than his sister; he will grow up to be attracted to girls; he will be tough; he will not cry if he gets hurt; and he will want to hunt and fish and do all the other things his culture associates with being a man.

When children depart from these gender expectations in some way, parents tend to become nervous. Is there something wrong with my child? Will he or she get picked on at school? Have I raised my child wrong?

Imagine that same boy, brought up in a house surrounded by sports images and blue curtains, starting to ask his mother at the age of three if he can have a doll. Or wear a dress like his sister. Or put on mommy's lipstick. Or telling her that he wants to marry his best friend, who is also a boy. What are some ways his mom can respond? How would *you* respond? Or what if your child is one of the approximately fifteen thousand babies born each year in the United States who have indeterminate genitalia, classifying them as "intersex" or persons with a "disorder of sex development"?[1]

It is important even before their baby is born for parents to think about the ways in which they put labels and expectations on their child. We place a lot of hopes and dreams in our children, and gender is one way in which we lock them into certain dreams and categories that they may not have for themselves. In chapter 4, we will explore the challenges of gender and how science is showing us how much more complicated it is than we have tended to think about it. But for now, just consider how much gender is already a part of our society's expectations for a child's identity, even before they are born.

For the Birth Certificate: The Race of the Parents

Try and recall those months before and after the birth of your child or of another child you know. How did you think about the identity of that child? What questions did your child's birth certificate application require you to answer? If you look at your own birth certificate and your parents' and compare it to your

---

[1]Gerald Callahan, *Between XX and XY: Intersexuality and the Myth of Two Sexes* (Chicago: Chicago Review Press, 2009), 7. Nicholas Teich, *Transgender 101: A Simple Guide to a Complex Issue* (New York: Columbia University Press, 2012).

child's, you may notice differences. As a society, we change how we categorize people depending on what we think is important.

When I (Carolyn) was born, forty years ago, hospital officials recorded the race of my father and my mother on my birth certificate: "White." In the space next to the race question, there was a space for whether my mother and father were "Of Spanish Origin?" followed by "If Yes, Specify Mexican, Cuban, Puerto Rican, etc."

There is no race listed on my husband's birth certificate. He was born two years before me in Bangkok, Thailand. The certificate states the nationality of both of his parents as American, specifies that he does not qualify for Thai nationality, but does not ask for race.

When we had children, our race was not included on our children's birth certificates. I don't recall whether we had to answer questions about race and ethnicity on the application form, but on the official certificate we received, no race is listed.

When a baby is born, why might it be important to know the race of the parents? If we can make an assumption based purely on the fact of race appearing on a baby's birth certificate, then it was important in the United States in 1980, but not in Thailand in 1978, and it was no longer important in the first decade of the twenty-first century.

By 2016, the time of the most recent birth certificate questionnaire available on the Centers for Disease Control website, race and ethnicity had again become markers of identity, though the form insists that this information is being used for "research purposes only" and will not be included on the certificate itself.[2]

A new mother giving birth in the United States today is asked whether she is of Spanish origin, and if so, whether from Mexico, Puerto Rico, Cuba, or other (fill in the blank), followed by a question that asks her race. The boxes available to check in the race category include White, Black or African American, American Indian or Alaska Native (with a request for the tribe's name), Asian Indian,

---

[2]https://www.cdc.gov/nchs/data/dvs/moms-worksheet-2016-508.pdf.

Chinese, Filipino, Japanese, Korean, Vietnamese, Other Asian (with a request to specify), Native Hawaiian, Guamanian or Chamorro, Samoan, Other Pacific Islander (specify) and Other (specify). The question's instructions state to check one or more boxes.

Even though Spanish origin is seen as separate from race, the descriptor "Hispanic" continues to be used as a category that is distinct from White or Black. For instance, when looking up vital statistics for birth rates in the state of Texas, one can look at the data according to the race/ethnicity of the mother, and the options are White, Black, Hispanic, and Other.[3]

The categories of "race" and ethnicity continue to change and shift over time, but the way society interprets skin color continues to affect how persons are treated and also how persons themselves identify. In a study of Mexican Americans, sociologists Vilma Ortiz and Edward Telles state that Hispanic persons with darker skin report more experiences with racial discrimination than light-skinned Hispanics.[4] These authors also point out differences in how persons of Spanish origin identify as "Hispanic" or whether they connect to a culture that emphasizes this heritage: light-skinned Mexican Americans may choose the "White" box, and they may or may not choose to identify more closely with their Hispanic heritage later in life.[5]

The whole history of the label "Hispanic" is problematic. Prior to the Spanish colonizers coming to North America in the late fifteenth century, non-Spanish speaking indigenous people lived all across the continent. The Valley of Mexico surrounding the ancient capital city Tenochtitlán (what we now call Mexico City) was home to more than a million indigenous people during the Aztec Empire, before Spanish conquistador Hernán Cortés arrived and brought devastating sicknesses and armies and a different religion.[6] But

[3]http://healthdata.dshs.texas.gov/VitalStatistics/Birth.

[4]Vilma Ortiz and Edward Telles, "Racial Identity and Racial Treatment of Mexican Americans," *Race and Social Problems* 4, no. 1 (April 2012), https://www.ncbi.nlm.nih.gov/pmc/articles/PMC3846170/.

[5]Ortiz and Telles, "Racial Identity."

[6]Carrie Gibson, *El Norte: The Epic and Forgotten Story of Hispanic North America* (New York: Atlantic Monthly Press, 2019), 20.

the remaining descendants of indigenous peoples still live in areas across North America, and while many of them may now *speak* Spanish, they are not necessarily "Hispanic" or "of Spanish origin."

Additionally, Portuguese slave traders brought enslaved Africans to the Caribbean islands to work in the sugar cane fields, and many of their descendants still live in Haiti and the Dominican Republic as well as across Central and South America in countries such as Brazil. Many of these persons speak Spanish or Portuguese, and they have a variety of dark skin tones, much like other descendants of the African diaspora. Even though they may speak Spanish, calling these persons "Hispanic" or labeling them as being "of Spanish origin" does not do justice to their history.

For this reason, many people who have previously been labeled "Hispanic" prefer to identify as "Latino" or "Latina," or to use a term that includes both the male and female forms: "Latinx" (pronounced Latinex). And some persons prefer to be called by their land of origin: Mexican, Puerto Rican, Cuban, Dominican, and so on. The labels we give people are not necessarily the labels they would choose for themselves.

What Is "Identity"?

We established earlier that before a baby is even brought home from the hospital, the identity categories of gender and race are already applied to the child, and that these categories of identity tell us something about our cultural surroundings. Our history and culture affect our concepts of race and national origins, our ideas about gender, and beliefs regarding our sexual orientation.

These markers of identity and categories of diversity are not static across the generations. Unlike letters of the alphabet that may be engraved on blocks that parents can pass down through generations, the language of diversity and labels of identity do change. The alphabet or basic building blocks for what we need to teach our kids about diversity is something we must continue to relearn ourselves. What we know now and what we believe about identity, our own parents may not have known or believed when they were raising us, and what our children believe when they are old enough to have their own children will in turn be different from what we believe now.

Kwame Anthony Appiah, a professor of philosophy and law at New York University, wrote a book tellingly titled *The Lies That Bind,* which discusses how identity functions in society.[7] Appiah writes that identities "come, first, with labels and ideas about why and to whom they should be applied. Second, your identity shapes your thoughts about how you should behave; and, third, it affects the way other people treat you."[8] The essential questions around identity involve "who" as well as "what" you are, and these answers affect both your own behavior as well as the behavior of others toward you.

Appiah knows these kinds of questions from personal experience. As he travels, he is constantly being asked "Where are you *from?*" And the question, he understands, is not simply about the place where he currently lives or the city in which he was born (London), but rather where his "people" come from. This is a complicated question to answer for Appiah, who is the son of an Englishwoman with roots going back to the thirteenth century in Britain, and of a Ghanaian father who can trace his ancestry back to an eighteenth-century general who helped establish the Asante Empire. With roots in Africa and England, people he meets around the world mistake him for someone from India, Brazil, Ethiopia, and several other different countries. Given his appearance, people are surprised to find he speaks with a British accent.

The labels and ideas that go along with identity markers help us group people into categories and make some sense of the world. In some ways, they serve a function as we learn about the world. For babies entering the developmental stage of "separation anxiety," in which they show signs of distress when not in the arms of their primary caregiver, a basic set of internal labels helps them identify who is their caregiver and who is not. As children grow older and create friendships, labels affect who they consider an "insider" and

---

[7]Kwame Anthony Appiah, *The Lies That Bind: Rethinking Identity* (New York: Liveright Publishing, 2018).
[8]Appiah, *The Lies That Bind,* 12.

an "outsider," to whom they will extend hospitality, and whom they want to keep out.

Identity Markers: Essentializing and Bias

Categories of identity help us to make meaning, but they also limit our understanding. For instance, when we use identity categories to *essentialize* every person within that category as having the same characteristics, we are limiting our understanding of the diversity of human individuals. Appiah calls out essentialism as the act of assuming "superficial differences [or categories of identity]— the ones that lead to applying the label—reflect deeper, inward differences that explain a great deal of how people behave."[9] To essentialize is to say that because someone fits into a category of identity, then they must share particular qualities with all others in that same category. An example of essentialism is to say that all girls love dolls, or that all Italians love pasta.

When society makes these categories into essential attributes, or sees all persons in that category as having the same qualities, then people in that group are treated based on those assumptions, whether good or bad. The discussion of "implicit bias," or the ways people make unconscious decisions about others on a daily basis, gets at this pattern of essentializing people according to their identity groups.[10]

In her book *Biased: Uncovering the Hidden Prejudice that Shapes What We See, Think, and Do,* Stanford professor of psychology Jennifer Eberhardt writes that people make multiple associations with different characteristics, including age, weight, accent, disability, and height.[11] She focuses on race because of the long history of black people being associated with crime, highlighting the devastating effect this has had on African American individuals and communities. But she says that "stereotyping is universal...

---

[9]Appiah, *The Lies That Bind,* 26.

[10]You can take your own implicit bias test at https://implicit.harvard.edu/implicit/.

[11]Jennifer Eberhardt, *Biased: Uncovering the Hidden Prejudice that Shapes What We See, Think, and Do* (New York: Viking, 2019), 7.

However, the content of those stereotypes is culturally generated and culturally specific."[12]

The context in which a child grows up determines the kind of prejudices and biases that child will hold. *Even if you see yourself as not biased, your child is picking up biases all the time.* For instance, researchers from the University of Washington showed videos to preschoolers in which different adults were treated differently. In one video, the adult was treated warmly and freely offered a toy; in another, the adult received negative attention and was given a toy only reluctantly.[13] Afterwards, the preschoolers were asked to which adult they themselves would give the toy. The majority of children said they would give the toy to the adult who received the positive treatment in the video. The implication of this choice is that children model the behavior they see in the adults around them, even if those adults are not their own caregivers. If an adult treats a person badly, a child is likely to view the person who receives the bad treatment as somehow to blame and deserving of that treatment.

Early on, children notice persons being treated badly, whether it is someone being made fun of or teased, or simply being treated with indifference as compared with another who is warmly greeted and welcomed. Children make meaning out of these observations, tending to attribute blame to the persons treated badly rather than to the person who is acting badly. Children notice how the adults around them treat other people, and they make assumptions about categories of people based on how they are treated.

How to Respond to Bias: Knowing Ourselves

Perhaps you are someone who has experienced biased treatment from others, and those experiences have affected how you view

---

[12]Eberhardt, *Biased,* 35.

[13]Allison Skinner, Andrew N. Meltzoff, and Kristina R. Olson, "'Catching' Social Bias: Exposure to Biased Nonverbal Signals Creates Social Biases in Preschool Children," *Psychological Science* 28, no. 2 (2017): 216–224. Available online: https://www.researchgate.net/profile/Andrew_Meltzoff/publication/316630264_ Catching_social_bias_Exposure_to_biased_nonverbal_signals_creates_ social_biases_in_preschool_children/links/5908ad10a6fdcc496163e74d/ Catching-social-bias-Exposure-to-biased-nonverbal-signals-creates-social-biases-in-preschool-children.pdf. Cited in Jennifer Eberhardt, *Biased,* 35.

your identity. But experiencing bias does not necessarily determine *how* we then view our identity. Maybe experiencing prejudicial treatment makes you want to downplay your association with your religious background, or maybe it makes you more vocal about your faith to counteract stereotypes. Our reaction to bias is not dependent on our identity because our experiences are different, as are the meanings we each attach to those experiences.

Appiah offers us this insight: "While your identity affects your experience, there's no guarantee that what you've learned from it is going to be the same as what other people of the same identity have learned."[14] We may share things in common with other people who have experienced the kind of discrimination we ourselves have gone through, and yet we also may not.

While sitting in San Antonio with several black college students from New York City who came to conduct oral history interviews, I (Carolyn) overheard one talking about a conservative panelist they heard that morning at the conference. A local radio DJ who is black came and spoke to the group of students, most of whom were from HBCUs (Historically Black Colleges and Universities). Apparently, in the panel conversation the DJ had made some political remarks. Afterwards, the students from New York were sharing with one another: "That's the first conservative black person I've ever met!" Even though they shared the same skin color and received similar forms of discrimination by society, these students and this DJ did not share the same political viewpoints.

An important first step in responding to bias is understanding your own identity better and how your experiences have been shaped by biases toward that identity. How have you been treated differently than others in society because of your gender? race? nationality? accent? physical abilities? height? weight? hair? age? occupation? faith? politics? education? state and place of residence?

Our identity can encompass a number of different facts and traits about us—sports teams we like, whether we like cats or dogs, whether we consider ourselves a night owl or a morning person, how we introduce ourselves, and our hobbies and interests. Some

[14]Appiah, *The Lies That Bind*, 20.

of these traits are ones we choose; others are given at birth or are
assigned to us by our surrounding culture. All of these can be part of
our identity. Each of these qualities makes us similar to others who
also share these characteristics. Taken together, they make up the
uniqueness of each of us as individuals. Some parts of our identity
matter more to some people than to others, and which ones matter
may depend upon the audience.

Understanding the various components of our own identity
helps us recognize when aspects of our identity seem to matter
more in some contexts, and which aspects give us prestige or
perhaps target us for discrimination. By knowing that parts of our
identity are more valued in some settings than others, we can begin
to see how society reacts to those different parts of who we are.
That may also help us become more aware of when others are being
overlooked or marginalized because of some parts of their identity.

In the first Appendix at the end of the book, each of us authors
have written our own "autobiography of culture," an example of
what it might look like to unpack some of what makes each of us
unique.

Carolyn Shares: Parts of My Identity

While I (Carolyn) haven't always embraced my identity as a
"woman," over time I have come to see how society sends subtle
(and not so subtle) messages that devalue women. I grew up as the
fifth of six children, and as the youngest girl before the only boy
in the family. Upon hearing that I have four older sisters, some
persons have remarked, "Your parents must have kept trying until
they got a boy!" thinking themselves clever or original. My parents
did not "keep trying" for a boy, but they were glad to have all of
their daughters as well as their son. But even with supportive and
loving parents such as I have, I got the message from society: boys
are better.

Societies send these messages through their public policies, too.
For instance, in the United States, there is no paid maternity leave.
Upon giving birth, employees are allowed a twelve-week *unpaid*
leave, as required by federal law. Some companies offer employees

paid leave, but this is at their discretion. In other words, society values my identity as a worker and producer, except when that work and production have to do with giving birth to a baby. Only one in five women has access to paid maternity leave after a birth or adoption.[15]

Being a woman in another context also shapes how society treats me: as a preaching professor. Because I teach in a field dominated by men (preaching), and in a time when the majority of Christians around the world still do not see women as having biblical authority to preach, some students see my gender as a reason to dismiss what I have to say.

But whether or not I like the identity "woman," it is part of the identity that society has assigned to me, bringing with it the baggage of negative connotations that our society has made with women: overly emotional, maternal (for better or worse), either likeable and easy to get along with or a word that starts with a "b" and sounds like witch.

I am also white. I do not like that we live in a racist society based on racializing some people as "white" and others as "black" or "brown," but society has deemed me white, and that is part of my identity too. And because I have learned that being white means that I am unfairly advantaged in society and am often given access to people and resources not available to people of color, I have come to see my white identity as being very important to who I am, because it means that I have a responsibility to try and make a difference in an unfair system.

Society's Views on Identity Shift over Time

Identity is complex. There are parts of it that are easy to talk about, and other parts that make it an uncomfortable subject for "polite" dinner conversation. Identity is not static; we do not stay the same. And neither is our society. The way our society responds to particular identities changes over time.

---

[15]Haley Swenson, "What Is the Future of Paid Parental Leave in America?" *Pacific Standard*, April 2, 2019, https://psmag.com/social-justice/the-future-of-paid-parental-leave-in-america.

For example, in a span of fifteen years, a large portion of the United States population experienced a complete reversal in their views on same-sex marriage. In 2004, 60 percent of persons polled were against legalizing same-sex marriage and only 31 percent were for it; in 2019 those numbers reversed.[16] Supporters of same-sex marriage are still largely politically affiliated with Democrats (75 percent of persons who identify as Democrat or Democrat-leaning, compared with only 44 percent of persons who identify as Republican or Republican-leaning, support gay marriage), but there are more than twice as many people who are Republican who support same-sex marriage as there were fifteen years ago (44 percent of Republicans in 2019, compared with 19 percent in 2004).[17]

What this means is that different parts of our identities matter differently, and at different times, to different people. Again, this is complicated. But if we can start to name identities and their impact on our society, then we can address the harmful stereotypes that do real damage to groups and individuals. The activities that follow help with this.

Chapter 2 Activity for Self-Reflection

Autobiography of Identities

As quickly as you can, list the ways you describe yourself to another person. What are the components of your identity that matter the most to you? Which parts do you think about the most? the least? Is there any aspect of your identity that you do not feel society values? Write about any of your earliest memories pertaining to the most salient parts of your identity: What were the circumstances; what messages did you hear either explicitly or implicitly; how did that make you feel?

Reflecting on the *ABCs of intentional engagement* (see chapter 1), when did you first *acknowledge* this particular part of your identity? Are you able to *be present* to any feelings that this part of your

---

[16]David Masci, Anna Brown, and Jocelyn Kiley, "5 Facts about Same-Sex Marriage," *Pew Research,* 24 June 2019, https://www.pewresearch.org/fact-tank/2019/06/24/same-sex-marriage.

[17]Masci, Brown, and Kiley, "5 Facts."

identity brings up for you? Can you *come closer* to this part of your identity, reflecting more on it or perhaps connecting with others who share this part of your identity?

Take some time to think about the *interpersonal ABCs of a more just society*. What parts of your identity give you *access* to certain resources or communities because you share an identity that society values? Is there a way you can share that access with persons who do not have the benefit of that shared identity? Can you *build* opportunities to connect with people who share an identity with you that society has not valued, and by building connections help to offer one another support? Finally, *cultivate* within yourself habits of gratitude and courage, reflecting on the things you have learned because of these different parts of who you are.

3

Identity and Diversity in Action

Joy Shares: Kids on a Train

Recently, I took my son to a prep school evaluation event. We live in Queens, and the closest school to us is underfunded and underperforming, so we were looking into other options for our children, including prep schools. After a tiring day, we boarded the Long Island Railroad to return home. As we looked for seats, I saw a man with a stroller that held a sleeping child. He was sitting on the end of a section of seats, so I asked if he wouldn't mind moving briefly so my son and I could slide in and sit next to the window. His other child, also a boy, saw my son—and there was an instant attraction between the two kids. They realized they were pretty much the same—they identified each other as the same gender, were of about the same height…and that was all that mattered! We also found out during the ride that their birthdays are literally a month apart. The boys became fast friends on the ride home. This prompted us parents to have a conversation; his wife was sitting across the aisle because their older son, the one playing with my son, went back and forth between his parents.

We began talking about the expense of raising children, extracurricular activities, and that we both knew what it felt like for people to have the audacity to ask us if we were having another child. Yes, in theory I suppose it would be nice to have another child, I said, as both my husband and I come from families of three siblings. But *given the state of our bank account*—nope. Then the conversation moved to education and school because what else could parents of young children possibly have to talk about?

I mentioned my decision *not* to send my son to universal pre-K offered for free in New York City. They echoed the challenge of getting into a universal pre-K in their area but acknowledged that at least they seem to have options of good public schools. They live on the Upper West Side, and after a slightly challenging time with pre-K, they were able to get their son into a *good* public school program. After being on a waiting list or two, they ended up at a school within walking distance of their home, and of course their youngest child will eventually end up at the same school because of the sibling rule. Living on the Upper West Side has its privileges…I guess…maybe.

They listened to my story as well. I had applied to non-zoned public schools. I did not apply to the closest neighborhood school, but nonetheless the New York City Public Schools sent me a letter congratulating me on the fact that my son had been offered a seat there. I was hurt, dumbfounded. Why invite me to *apply* to other schools under the guise of choice and then, without having received an application to it, simply offer my son a seat at the closest school? I sent an email. They responded that it had to do with making sure every child has a seat, and that we were still waitlisted for the other schools to which we had applied.

I said to the parents on the train, "We don't have those options in Queens. So I will apply to the independent schools and to a few charter schools." I wish I could send my children to the neighborhood school. It would be convenient. But I would definitely have to do damage control, and since I've been a public school teacher, I know that in most cases damage control—after it has already been done—is like gambling. These are my children. I *invest* in them—I don't do *damage control*.

Exactly what we talked about next I can't recall, but the couple's son, who had crossed the aisle to his mother, asked what I had said. The father started speaking to him in an Asian language, which I couldn't quite figure out. It didn't sound like Chinese or Japanese, neither did he look like either of those ethnicities. After the father finished talking, the mother started speaking a completely different language to the boy. I knew she was white and I was trying to figure it out—*ear hustlin'*. It seemed somewhat familiar, but sitting across the aisle I was too far away, and the train too loud, for me to be sure. I sat in amazement for a second that this five-year-old boy clearly spoke or at least understood three languages. I leaned over to him and asked, "Did you get all that?" His parents laughed. Turns out he understands Vietnamese, German, and English. What a combination! I couldn't help but think that this is what America is becoming—in a good way. It was not just one group that seemed to be increasing but also people of different ethnicities and cultures who marry and raise children who come from different worlds—the world of their parents and the world in which they live. I couldn't help but be reminded of the young lady I had met at a workshop a few months earlier who was Israeli and Haitian. This is what it means to live in the United States of America nowadays. Diversity is all around us.

Growing Pains

This picture of two young boys "crossing the aisle" on a train conveys a sense of ease, of getting along happily with people who are different from ourselves, but we know this is not always the case. Both children and adults can have a hard time getting comfortable with people who are different from them. As a society, we have tended to be suspicious of difference. And yet difference is all around us. But getting used to difference can be a kind of "growing pain" experienced on a personal and societal level.

We all have growing pains. We experience them differently at different times in our lives. Some of us experience the pain of our limbs stretching, trying to conform to the map that our genetics have laid out.

Sometimes the growing pains come from having to handle a situation on our own, or realizing that we cannot control the behavior of others, or that there are always consequences for the decisions we make—good, bad, or just plain frustrating.

Although growing pains can be challenging, might we reframe them and consider them liberating instead? Growing pains mean that there is movement, life, and that one is not stuck or stagnant— or dead. Growing pains can signal or mean that there is still a chance, an opportunity, hope.

When we interact with people who are different from us, and we feel awkward, this too is a kind of growing pain. There is growth in that moment. And it is also uncomfortable, which is why we call such growth *painful*.

Our communities, our nation, and our world are experiencing growing pains. As challenging as that may be for us, as uncomfortable as we may be at times, there is still hope. For there is life, and it is this *life* on which we must focus.

As Old as Time

As long as humans have existed on the face of the earth, for various reasons we have organized ourselves into groups based on similarities and differences. From a human developmental standpoint, long before race, ethnicity, socioeconomic class, gender, and sexuality significantly enter the picture, children often group themselves according to likes and dislikes of, say, ice cream and cartoons. Grouping, or the organization of people into groups based on a particular characteristic, or even several, is not new. It's a practice as old as time.

Old too is diversity. If we think about it, ever since people have been in contact with others through trade and exploration and war, people have had contact with difference. Human beings have been sharing the planet for more than 350,000 years! In that span of time, humans most certainly made mistakes, committed wrongs, and on occasion formed positive relationships. In times past, people were able to stay in their own groups. Contact with others was limited and based upon time, geography, and economic means, just as it is today. Now, however, these obstacles are not as challenging as they once were. Our ability to connect and stay connected is easily facilitated through mediated communication.

We have access to one another in ways that are so powerful, and in some instances, *free*. Today, at least in the United States, one can go to any major city and never have to board a plane to experience another culture or tradition. We are influenced by one another in ways we do not realize—think about the food or music you encounter that is different from your own cultural or ethnic context.

We know from geography and other historical sources that humans move—migrate—from one place to another for various reasons (such as war, famine, employment, and for medical services). Pick any cultural or ethnic group you like, and if you poke around in their history you will find that at some point: 1) they may have migrated for one reason or another, and 2) they connected by choice or force with another cultural group. So while humans have always grouped themselves, they have also maintained contact to varying degrees with those who are different from them, and sometimes with much success.

Another consistent aspect of human behavior is an aversion to change. Sure, we have to deal with change because it is part of our existence, but many of us would keep things the same if we had a choice. We often refer to such sameness as tradition.

The Role of Tradition: Our Stories of Origin

There are many people who love tradition, even worship it. One of the reasons we like tradition is that *it helps us identify and solidify our story*, or at least the story we've been told.

Stories remind us of our identity. Stories—or narratives—tell us who we are, where we came from, and who we are in relation to other people. Narratives are the first type of literature that we learn as children, and it is not until we are in the third or fourth grade that the narrative is put aside (temporarily) and replaced with informational text. This movement can be a hard shift for some children to make, and it can be just as hard for adults.

Think about it. From the time we are born, we are fed stories or narratives about various characters. Stories help us to connect with our world. There are lessons embedded within them, and they are powerful. Do you remember what your favorite story was as a child? What did that story do for you then? What does it do for you now? What about your child: What is his or her favorite story? Why do you think we even have favorites?

Stories, or narratives, are a source of tradition. Tradition is and can be a beautiful thing, but it can also be hostile and unforgiving. Therefore, we submit to you, dear reader, that tradition loses its value when it cannot deal with or adapt to the changes that occur in human existence, and when it is not steeped in the truth. Tradition should *connect us* to our past *but not hold us hostage* in our present. And it should represent the truth.

Traditions can be "stories of origin," or what we believe about where our ancestors came from or our family's country of origin. These are the big stories we tell ourselves about how we got to be where we are and who we are today. We often pass on these stories like a tradition. And yet these stories usually point out only the heroes in our past, not the villains, and can leave out important information. We typically do not retell stories that depict us in a negative way.

If we are not careful, our devotion to tradition and story can—and often does—also lead us to fear. When we are scared, we attempt to protect that which we believe, or feel, is ours—right or wrong. This fear is exemplified in the things we think, say, and do to one another.

Just as each individual person has his or her own faults and virtues, so too do entire societies. By remaining open to seeing how our society has had faults and continues to have faults, we identify where we can each work in the struggle to make our society and world better together.

The Reality of Diversity

In 1990, I (Joy) was in the eighth grade. An article came out in *Time* magazine that caused a stir. It spoke about the increasing diversity that could be seen and felt in places like my middle-class neighborhood and school in Queens, N.Y. That was thirty years ago. With prophetic-like accuracy the words in this article ring true today. "Americans are more racially and ethnically diverse than in the past, and the US is projected to be even more diverse in the coming decades."[1] There are challenges to becoming a more diverse country, a more diverse world. In the United States, what it means to be an American is up for redefinition. This is what cultural shifts entail.

Also in that *Time* article, historian Thomas Beder said, "If the center cannot hold, then one must redefine the center."[2] Indeed, the center *is* being redefined. Molefi Asante, professor at Temple University, said it best thirty years ago: "Once America was a microcosm of European nationalities...Today, America is a microcosm of the world."[3]

Like we said, diversity is a good thing, but it has its challenges.

Demographer William Frey acknowledges that there are challenges to diversity (and might we add, intercultural communication), and yet he also recognizes the need to celebrate it.[4] This is what it means to respect the differences and honor the similarities. Frey explains that without this *new blood*, the nation's labor force would decline and the national population would stagnate.

Both the challenges and the reasons to celebrate diversity should be handled with care. Frey uses the term *demographic turbulence*—but he and we need a change of mind, or paradigm here. Demographic change does not have to be negative. Frey believes that in fact there will be a shift in perspective, because diversity is tied up with America's social and economic future. Currently, the reason for the divide is that folks do not recognize their connection or connectedness to one another. It looks like there is one set of concerns for the older, predominantly white generation and another set of concerns for the younger, more diverse generations. However, as Frey demonstrates in his text, diversity is the key to our

---

[1] William Henry, III, "Beyond the Melting Pot," *Time*, April 9, 1990.
[2] Henry, "Beyond the Melting Pot."
[3] Henry, "Beyond the Melting Pot."
[4] William Frey, *Diversity Explosion* (Washington, D.C.: The Brookings Institution, 2018).

social and economic future. As people begin to see this and reckon with it, their perspective will shift on the issues of diversity and on socioeconomics as well. However, fear of the unknown currently stands guard in the hearts and minds of many across our country.

Fear keeps us from talking and engaging authentically. Fear has revealed our true but often hidden feelings that have been covered up by political correctness. The reality that scares many people is that they are not sure where this new wave of globalization will lead. Some see this as a watershed moment. Watershed moments are critical, pivotal moments that have a profound effect—and these effects last for a long time.

Let me say it loud for the folks in the back of the room: *We are living in a diverse country, a diverse world! There is no going back!* Although some people openly, or secretly, wish for this. Diversity, in all its forms, but especially ethnic diversity, is here to stay.

Dear reader, the stakes are high this time around, and this is something that we need to recognize, accept, and learn to navigate.

So what *is* different this time around? What exactly are the growing pains that we are experiencing as a nation?

Immigration

The first of several growing pains our nation is experiencing is immigration. The United States is a country founded by immigrants (the question of whether that founding was *legal* is a whole other story). The only persons that were here when immigrants first arrived were indigenous persons we have come to call Native Americans.

Immigration continues to be a hot topic in the government and in news media outlets. However, immigration is how we became the country we are today. Various people groups moved here in hopes of making a better life for themselves and their families, while others were forced to come here. Without immigration, you, and I, regardless of the context, simply would not be here having this conversation.

Looking at recent media content, especially about the forty-fifth presidency, one might think *recent* immigration is the source of many of the problems in the United States, and particularly that it is responsible for the uptick in diversity. However, that would be far from the truth. In actuality, immigration trends to the United States began to change over a generation ago, as early as the 1960s.[5]

Policies about immigration over the past century and a half have affected who can immigrate and from where. In the late nineteenth century, the United States prevented Chinese laborers from entering the country whereas before it had welcomed them, using them to build our railroads. In the early twentieth century, the government put caps on the number of immigrants that could come from certain countries, using a quota system. In 1965, the federal government did away with the race-and nationality-based quota system in the Immigration and Nationality Act.

Academics, research institutions, and media outlets have all noted the increase in diversity in the United States. For example, Jared Alcantara notes that general trends in immigration to the United States have changed over the last fifty years. In the 1960s immigration from Europe, Canada, and Oceania (Australia, New Zealand) accounted for 49 percent of U.S. immigrants. However, in 2013 immigrants from these countries accounted for approximately 12 percent of the United States immigrant population, whereas those from Latin America, Asia, and Africa accounted for just over 86 percent.[6]

In 2016, according to the Pew Research Center's article "10 Demographic Trends Shaping the U.S. and the World in 2016," "Nearly 59 million immigrants have arrived in the U.S. in the past 50 years, mostly from Latin America and Asia."[7] This statement alone helps us to see that America did not all of a sudden become a diverse country. People did not just magically appear. They have been coming for a long time!

---

[5]Frey, *Diversity Explosion*.

[6]Jared Alcantara, *Crossover Preaching: Intercultural-Improvisational Homiletics in Conversation with Gardner C. Taylor* (Downers Grove, Ill.: InterVarsity Press, 2015).

[7]D'Vera Cohn and Andrea Caumont, "10 Demographic Trends Shaping the U.S. and the World in 2016," *Pew Research*, March 31, 2016, https://www.pewresearch.org/fact-tank/2016/03/31/10-demographic-trends-that-are-shaping-the-u-s-and-the-world.

America is, and arguably *was*, predicated on such notions: diversity and freedom, and thus a self-fulfilling prophecy presents itself clearly at this moment in time.

William Frey, a demographer, also notes that diversity is now being seen not just in major gateway cities like New York City, Chicago, and Miami, but also in the Southeast, Mountain West, and states like Minnesota, from where United States Congresswoman and former Sudanese refugee Ilhan Omar hails. It is the "scattered parts of middle America [that] represents the front lines of the country's new diversity explosion."[8]

Diversity, in particular ethnic diversity, in the United States is not new. We do not have to look far in our nation's history. In just over the last generation we can see the shifts occurring, and we are living with those shifts today and will continue to live with these changes well into the twenty-second century and beyond. There is no way to undo what has been set in motion.

Now to be sure, there are other forms of diversity that can and will be addressed in other sections of this book. However, the way the United States Census counts people tends to be more concerned with ethnic (or national) origins.

While immigration is definitely a growing pain (in that the population of this country continues to grow in number), it is also one that has been present since the inception of this nation. The statue of Liberty still stands...and the huddled masses continue to come, generation after generation. The scope of this book cannot accommodate a thorough look at immigration policy, but we do hope to reframe immigration as an asset and benefit to this country. Currently, this "growing pain" actually aids the United States by replenishing its aging workforce, adding to the population, and connecting this country to other places around the world.

As we try to wrap our minds around these shifts in population, we must also deal with the growing pains of an aging workforce. In the aforementioned article, Pew notes that number ten on its list of demographic trends is that the population is aging on a global and

---

[8]Frey, *Diversity Explosion*, 28.

national scale. The article cites rapid population growth from 1950 to 2010 but projects that from 2010 to 2050 there is going to be a major slow-down in population growth.[9]

Demographer William Frey focuses more specifically on aging in the United States, noting that *white* baby boomers are retiring and the "continual loss of boomers from the labor force will slow its growth considerably...the white labor force–age population will decline by 15 million from 2010 to 2030." People of color groups will contribute to the gains in the workforce population by 24 million.[10]

Generational Differences

We also begin to see this divide along generational fault lines. David Livermore, in *Cultural Intelligence: Improving Your CQ to Engage Our Multicultural World,* lists generational culture as one of three major types of cultural domains. Cultural domain "refers to the various kinds of cultures and subcultures in which we find ourselves." [11] Besides generational culture, the two other domains are socioethnic and organizational (to what kind of social group you belong—an institution of higher learning, a place of employment, a church, a sports team, etc.).

Within our social groups, we have generational differences. When both generational and cultural/ethnic differences exist, the challenges are compounded. Younger generations are more diverse than ever before. So, we are dealing not only with generational differences, but differences between an aging and predominantly white generation and the most recent generation in which people of color outnumber whites. We see a good example of this kind of change from the 2018 election, where in the Democratic Congress more women and women of color were elected than ever before in our nation's history.

According to a 2019 article by Kasasa.com, a technology and financial firm, here is the latest generational breakdown. Baby

---

[9]Cohn and Caumont, "10 demographic trends."

[10]Frey, *Diversity Explosion,* 28.

[11]David Livermore, *Cultural Intelligence: Improving Your CQ to Engage Our Multicultural World* (Grand Rapids, Mich.: Baker Academic, 2009), 93.

Boomers are those born between 1944 and 1964. Generation X are those born between 1965 and 1979. Generation Y (Millennials) are those born between 1980 and 1994, and Generation Z are those born between 1995 and 2015.

Think about it: for baby boomers, the newly invented television in 1927 was a luxury that not every household could afford. Yet generation Z only knows cell phones, and high-definition (HD) television and tablets are standard. Clearly, there are cultural differences for these two generations in styles of communication preferred, issues that are important to them, and of course the typical generational battleground of music. This is just a small example of differences between "generational subcultures," as Livermore calls it, defining how persons from the same ethnic heritage but from different generations have vastly different experiences of the world.[12]

We experience diversity in myriad ways. However, ethnicity or race and generation cause the most pain and contention. The baby boom generation, which is predominantly white, has been a cultural and political driving force. This generation, like generations before, will decrease in number. The generations behind the baby boomer generation are increasingly more diverse ethnically or with ties to people of other cultures and languages. This will undoubtedly play out in national, state, and local elections over the next several decades.

Cultural Intelligence

To adjust to this growing pain, it is important for us to accept these changes as part of *growth* and learn how we can develop greater skills to interact with one another across these generational and cultural divides. For this, we turn to a new model of development called Cultural Intelligence.

In the past, our society has tried to measure our development or growth according to standard forms of measurement. We used IQ to measure a person's intellect. More recently, discussion has revolved around EQ, or Emotional Intelligence, acknowledging the

---

[12]Livermore, *Cultural Intelligence*, 102.

central role our emotions play in interpersonal relationships. Now, we must also attend to our CQ, our Cultural Intelligence.

Unlike IQ (intellect) and EQ (emotional intelligence), cultural intelligence is not a simple number on an exam. Cultural intelligence refers to the "capability to function effectively across various cultural contexts (national, ethnic, organizational, generational, etc.)."[13]

Within the Cultural Intelligence framework, there are four CQ capabilities. The first is CQ Drive. This capability is about your interest, motivation, and confidence to work in multicultural situations. Essentially, the question is, How interested are you in being around those who are different from you? Do you enjoy cultural difference? Does it give you pause? Do you experience angst or anxiety when around persons who are different? How motivated are you to learn about others who are different from you?

The second capability is CQ Knowledge, which looks at your knowledge base regarding how cultures are similar and different. What do you know about cultures in the West or the East? What experiences do you have with engaging people who are different from you? What movies or cultural references or artifacts affect how you engage with persons who are different from you? On what stereotypes are you relying to base your knowledge about others?

Of course, knowledge is not the only capability that is important: CQ Action looks at your ability to adapt when relating and working interculturally. Are you able to shift in your communication style to aid in productive and effective communication with those who are different from you?

The fourth portion of this framework is called CQ Strategy. This capability looks at your awareness and ability to plan in multicultural interactions: your ability to plan ahead and prepare for situations, in addition to reflecting on how well the communicative encounter transpired after the fact.

Cultural intelligence is a skill that we, and our progeny, must develop.

---

[13]Soon Ang and Linn Van Dyne, "Conceptualization of Cultural Intelligence," in *Handbook of Cultural Intelligence: Theory, Measurement, and Applications* (Armonk, N.Y.: M.E. Sharpe, 2008), 3.

It is developmental. It can change over time. It can be improved. The goal is not to increase a score but rather to increase one's skill and one's ability to communicate effectively with others across differences. There are many frameworks that can help with improving our intercultural communication. However, the cultural intelligence framework has been used all over the world and across industries. More importantly, it is developmental, so there is always room to grow.

Winning Together

From a technological perspective, we have been drawn in close—like when an athletic team huddles in for a pep talk or encouragement right before going on the field. They are close, touching. They know and are known. They can read one another, *nonverbally*, without words. They have a language, a dialect that the other team may not understand, and this gives them the advantage on the field. This is what technology has done for us as a community, as a nation, and as a world. It has brought us close together. But there are many different teams, or groups, on the field of life. Some people champion better healthcare, others the environment, some focus on education, and so on.

But we cannot stick only to our own groups or areas of focus. If we are going to move forward, we need to do more than just huddle in our own groups. We have to learn how to work together to *win!* Winning is not beating the other team at a game of *friendly* competition. No, winning is learning how to work with others so that when you huddle up at work or at your religious gathering and your teammate does not look like you, you already know how to navigate the similarities and differences in order to accomplish your group's goal.

Unfortunately, we cannot expect that the next generation will take on the task of learning how to engage differences and solve the challenges that society faces today. Certainly, they are smart enough and open enough. But they need our help and active involvement. This is why children have parents, students have teachers, and there are facilitators in workshops. Guides help people navigate the space—whether it is familiar or not. Scholars from across various fields, like seers of old, have said time and time again that the tides would change—and now here we are. The "new world is here. It is now. And it is irreversibly America."[14]

Chapter 3 Activity for Self-Reflection

Naming Our Own Growing Pains

Looking back over the ideas from this chapter about population shifts in the United States, immigration, generational differences, and the need for cultural intelligence, were there any moments where you felt uncomfortable while reading? Have you had any "growing pains" related to learning about new populations of people? Take a minute to consider your own triggers for the *automatic ABCs* of being **a**fraid, **b**acking away, and **c**ontrol. Did some of the topics bring up any feelings of fear for you? Sometimes the ways our world is changing can feel scary and overwhelming. Did you ever have the impulse to *back away*, or even put the book down? Think about your own social circle. Are you aware of any attempts (your own or others' on behalf of a community) to *control* the amount of diversity in your environment? How do the people around you talk about issues of immigration and changes in the population?

Write down your own responses, and then bring the *ABCs of intentional engagement* to these subjects. How does it feel to *acknowledge* your own responses to these topics? How can you *be present* to your feelings, and be present to the differences that these population shifts represent? Is there some way you can *come closer* to persons who have first-hand experience of these kinds of shifts?

Moving toward the *interpersonal ABCs of diversity*, what do these subjects have to do with *access*? How do some people gain access to the resources they need to support themselves and their families? Are there ways you can *build* bridges with persons from different backgrounds? And how might you *cultivate* an environment to help all persons thrive?

---

[14]Henry, *"Beyond the Melting Pot."*

4

Disentangling Gender and Sexuality

Joy Shares: Kids Say the Darndest Things

Recently, after picking up my children from school as usual, and arriving at our apartment building elevator, I realized someone was already in there waiting to go up, so we hurried. The person could have been read as being of either gender—male or female. Though the individual had a small beard underneath the chin, having had a nurse for a mom I knew that women lose estrogen as they age, and it can lead to things like increased hair growth. Anyways, the person, whom I believed to be a female, spoke. She sounded like she could be female, although there was a possibility the individual could be male. She was pleasant but I could tell my children were confused. My son smiled, spoke, and then looked at me. My daughter, like a typical three-year-old, with hand in mouth stared at the person.

We exchanged neighborly pleasantries as we got off at the first floor and both children said goodbye. I could tell the neighbor was endeared to them for the moment. But as we walked to our door and while I was looking for my keys—*and* before the elevator doors closed—my son asked loudly, "Mom, is that a boy or a girl?"

I figured the person in the elevator had to have heard his question. It was a legitimate one. I was embarrassed and felt bad. Not for my son's question, but for our neighbor. Everything my son has learned up till that moment had explicitly and *implicitly* told him that boys and girls, men and women, look a certain way, but this particular individual did not match with that information. So he was confused.

My feelings went out to the person on the elevator because I thought, "How many times has this question been asked? How does it make him or her feel?" I did not want to answer my son's question, partly because I realized I *could* be wrong.

What was most important to me, and what I wanted my children to take away from that encounter, was that this person is a human being. She or he was pleasant and neighborly in the elevator, we were the same, and that was all that mattered.

I was also tired, and still looking for the key, when my son, undeterred by my silence, asked again: "Mommy, is that a boy or girl?" Thankfully, by this time the elevator doors had closed.

Having a teaching background comes in handy in situations like this. I turned the question to him. I asked, "What do *you* think?" My bright boy said, "I think that was woman." I said, "I think you're right." I had found my keys and turned the lock.

We were finally home, and I was satisfied with the teaching moment that had just occurred. I realized that my answering the question could be misleading and that a long answer was not what was needed in this moment. I also trusted that he had enough information to come to a conclusion on his own, and what I needed to do in the moment was to guide and affirm. Mission accomplished. I realized I had done the right thing as a parent and a teacher, without doing damage either to my son or the individual in the elevator, whoever *he* or *she* might be.

Think back to when you can first remember noticing differences between people. Most likely it happened before you can even remember. Young children become interested in the differences between boys and girls at a very early age. Even before we can talk, we put toys into such categories. Children are able to recognize a family member: someone who is part of the same family as me; and a stranger: someone who is from a different family. The same-as-me and different-from-me distinctions begin as young children look for comfort and nourishment from the persons most likely to offer them care. When children are two, they already respond by gestures or words to the question, "Are you a boy or a girl?" By the age of three, children point out differences in gender, racial identity, physical abilities, and language. They are already constructing their own sense of identity, and learning what makes them like others and different from others.

Carolyn Shares: The Game of "Guess Who?"

The other day I was in a waiting room with a friend of my daughter's, and the waiting room had a bunch of games to keep kids occupied. The game we chose out of the stack was one called "Guess Who?" by Hasbro. Each player has a game board with flaps of characters' faces on them, facing toward you and away from your opponent. To start the game, each player draws a character from a stack of cards, and then through the process of asking "yes or no" questions, each player tries to guess the name of the other player's character. Players take turns asking questions with yes or no answers, and their opponent's answer should help them narrow down the possible faces belonging to their opponent. The questions typically begin with one related to gender, such as "Is your person a boy?" If the opponent says "no," then you drop down the faces of the characters on your game board that are boys, leaving up only the girl characters that could possibly belong to your opponent. Then the other player gets to ask a question, and so on. The questions keep going, becoming more detailed: "Is your person bald? Does your person have red hair?" And so on.

So in this waiting room I played with my daughter's nine-year-old friend. She had eliminated all the other possibilities but one, and yet when she named who she thought my character was, she guessed incorrectly. After this intricate back-and-forth of narrowing down the possibilities, how could this have happened?

When I showed her my card, she said, "Oh. I thought that was a boy."

The person I had selected was a character named "Jess." Jess had dark skin and shoulder-length blond hair. My opponent told me she thought a dark area above the mouth of this character was a moustache, and since she knew boys could have long hair, she guessed it was a boy. With a name like "Jess," it could definitely be a girl or a boy. I had assumed that since the character had long eyelashes like the other female-appearing characters, and since the darkness above the mouth looked to me like smile lines and not facial hair, Jess was a girl.

The experience highlighted for me how soon children are taught to categorize people. They play a kind of "Guess Who?" all the time, whether through a board game or in real life whenever they meet someone new, as Joy's kids did that day in the elevator. Gender is among the quickest categories by which we identify people: Is this person a boy or a girl? While the identifying markers may vary (my nine-year-old game-player knew that boys could have long hair, for instance), there still are a number of characteristics we associate with different genders. And yet gender itself is a concept that we are only recently beginning to understand fully.

Gender Identity Development

Challenges to our ideas about gender start even before a child is born, as we learn more about the science of sex chromosomes and the variations in human biology. Contrary to the traditional understanding that XX chromosomes make a girl, and XY chromosomes make a boy, scientists can show us that these chromosomes do not always predict a baby's genitalia.

Gerald Callahan, author of *Between XX and XY: Intersexuality and the Myth of Two Sexes*, points to a dizzying array of human variety when it comes to gender. The letters XX and XY are the chromosomes within a human's DNA that we tend to associate with women and men, respectively. Usually, if someone's DNA includes two X chromosomes, then the child will have female genitalia; and if one X and one Y are present, then the baby will have male genitalia. But Callahan points out that more than 65,000 people are born every year who, by those categories, are neither definitively boys or girls.[1] As a pathologist familiar with many other kinds of differences that exist among humans, including disorders that

---

[1]Gerald Callahan, *Between XX and XY: Intersexuality and the Myth of Two Sexes* (Chicago: Chicago Review Press, 2009), xi.

affect even fewer people than this number, Callahan was surprised that he had never heard much about this population. His research into this group of people evolved into his book *Between XX and XY*.

Throughout the book, Callahan explores the many biological influences upon our genitalia, including hormones and chromosomal differences, and he also names the varieties that exist in nature. Certain species of fish—including the cute clownfish on which Pixar's movie character *Nemo* is based—can change from female to male, and even back to female, with no change in the quality of their reproductive capacities.[2] Our ideas of male and female as being distinct and "opposite" sexes do not conform to the reality that can be found in nature.

Other human cultures also recognize this diversity in gender. In India, there are people known as *hijras*, who are identified as male when they are born but who grow up to dress and act like women and who often have a special celebratory role at the time of a baby's birth.[3] *Hijras* are recognized by the Indian government, enabling persons to identify as male, female, or as a third-gender if they prefer.[4] Other cultures around the world include different expressions of gender, including the people known as *phuying prophet song* or *kathoey* of Thailand, or the two-spirit people within certain Native American communities.[5]

These varieties point to the cultural embeddedness of our ideas around gender and sexuality. While some people insist on categories of gender as being "natural" and not variable across cultures, even science tells us that what is in "nature" is not always clear-cut male or female. Our ideas and expectations about gender and sex have a lot to do with our culture, and as our culture becomes more diverse, we need to reevaluate our ideas about gender.

---

[2] Callahan, *Between XX and XY*, 112.

[3] Callahan, *Between XX and XY*, 145.

[4] Kwame Anthony Appiah, *The Lies That Bind: Rethinking Identity* (New York: Liveright Publishing, 2018),11. Appiah cites the 2014 *Report of the Expert Committee on the Issues Relating to Transgender Persons* (Ministry of Social Justice and Empowerment, Government of India), Appendix 2, http://socialjustice.nic.in/writereaddata/UploadFile/Binder2.pdf.

[5] Nicholas Teich, *Transgender 101: A Simple Guide to a Complex Issue* (New York: Columbia University Press, 2012), 72–73.

Definitions and Key Terms

Some of the ways we are rethinking gender today come with the help of people like Callahan whose research on people with ambiguous genitalia help us understand the varieties of ways in which sex and gender manifest in humans. One of the earliest recorded medical histories of an intersex individual comes from 1952. A person named Lenore was labeled a girl at birth, after being born with what appeared to be obvious signs of female genitalia, but who actually had both X and Y chromosomes as well as undescended testes inside her abdomen.[6] Lenore's experiences and that of many others are helping us see that our simple categories of male or female don't mesh with the complexities of reality.

Other sources for learning about gender in new ways come directly from the people who are most affected: authors and scholars who do not identify with the gender they were assigned at birth. Nicholas Teich, a transman labeled female at birth, is a licensed social worker, founder of a camp for transyouth, and author of *Transgender 101: A Simple Guide to a Complex Issue*. The book's chapters describe ongoing debates within the world of transgender persons and advocates. For instance, Teich clarifies that the group of people that have some atypical sexual development or chromosomal combinations are called *intersex*, which is not exactly the same as *transgender*. For instance, many intersex people may use the term "disorders of sex development" to describe the challenges of living with genitalia that do not align with a single gender.[7] On the other hand, persons who are *transgender* may have been born with genitalia that typically identify them as male or female, but who grow up with the distinct feeling that this is not their true *gender*. In the case of Teich, he was labeled "female" at birth but identified as male.

Sex and gender are both more confusing and more complicated than we tend to think. As we can learn from intersex people, sex is not always male or female. In the case of persons who are transgender,

---

[6]Callahan, *Between XX and XY*, 1–7.
[7]Teich, *Transgender 101*, 133.

the sense of being a "girl" or a "boy" does not necessarily go along with the reproductive organs that appear as part of a person's body.

Persons who are transgender often know at a very young age that they do not "fit" in their bodies. When parents learn that their biological boy is actually a girl and wants to be called a girl's name, it can come as a shock and surprise, but support from parents typically helps the child emotionally in growing up and developing. The alternative—being forced to live as the gender assigned to one's sex—has been associated with higher levels of emotional stress, including depression and risk of suicide. For parents to be able to accept their child just as he or she is, as however they most identify, can literally be a matter of life or death.

Young children can also be *cisgendered*, or conforming to the gender they are assigned at birth, in other words, a person born with girl genitalia who feels like a girl and identifies as a girl. Identifying this category is helpful in that it makes clear that there are a number of different ways people can experience gender. Some persons may identify with the gender of their biological sex and also be *gender non-conforming*, which means, for example, that a person born a boy biologically sees himself as a boy but also likes to wear clothing typically associated with girls. A way a person identifies in terms of gender may be different from how they express themselves. Another way of saying this is that *gender identity* is different from *gender expression*.

What's Developmentally Appropriate?

Some parents and teachers may worry that talking with young children about differences related to sexual orientation or gender is not developmentally appropriate. But it is important to distinguish gender identity from sexual orientation. The two are not the same: Gender is about how one views oneself, and sexual orientation is about the gender of people to whom a person is attracted. A person may be born biologically a female, experience their own gender actually as a male, and later grow up to feel attraction toward men or women: a transman attracted to other men, or a transman attracted to women. A transwoman, labeled a boy at birth but who identifies as a woman, could grow up and marry another woman or a man. Talking about how people experience their own gender is not the same as talking about the gender to which each person finds him-, her-, or their-self attracted.

Another myth to dispel is the assumption that talking about sexual orientation involves speaking about sexual behavior. When teachers talk about families, they are not talking about sexual behavior among grown-ups. When teachers ask a child to talk about their mother and father, they are not implying that the children should speak about his or her parents' sexual relationship with one another. The parents are simply part of the child's family.

When a teacher talks about another child's two mommies, the teacher is not going to go into the dynamics of sexual behavior between adults. The teacher is talking about the composition of a child's family relationships. Naming the fact that some children come from households headed by people of the same gender does not mean talking about sexual behavior; it simply means naming the varieties of families in which children are raised in society.

Yet another related myth—that talking about LGBTQ people will somehow teach children to be gay—demonstrates a fear of gayness, or *homophobia*. To be afraid that teaching children about LGBTQ people will somehow make them "choose" to be gay also erroneously assumes that sexual orientation is a choice. Studies show that sexual orientation and gender identity are complex and are not determined by one element alone.[8] Rather than being afraid of what will happen when we introduce children to the variety of family constellations in the world, consider how this education benefits all children. Learning the differences of sexual orientation and gender identity among people enables children to make sense of the diverse world around them and helps deepen their capacity to be caring and supportive citizens and proud of who they are.

Sexuality and gender identity start forming at an early age. Children may begin talking about wanting to marry another child, and that person may be of the same or opposite gender. Children

---

[8]Simon LeVay, *Gay, Straight, and the Reason Why: The Science of Sexual Orientation*, 2d ed. (New York: Oxford University Press, 2017).

may get teased for playing with toys that other children see as gendered differently than the child who is playing with them: a boy playing with dolls? a girl playing with construction trucks? Children begin early on to forge identities around what is expected for their particular gender, and they make sure other kids adhere to the same rules for what boys and girls should each get to play with.

Parents cannot choose their children's gender or how their children identify in terms of gender. Parents cannot decide for their children which gender(s) their child will grow up to find attractive. But as parents, we can decide to support our children along the way. We can decide ahead of time to love our child as he or she or they are. And we can choose to educate persons in our communities in ways that can create inclusion and acceptance for persons who find themselves on different paths along this journey.

Presenting a Variety of Family Compositions

Adolescence is usually when parents have the "sex talk" with their children, or at least expect the school system to make education about sexuality available to their children. Having conversations with youth about sex can feel uncomfortable for parents, but we suggest it is first and foremost a parent's privilege and not a school's responsibility. This is also an opportunity for parents to talk to their children about gender identity and sexual orientation.

In some areas of the United States, there are numerous examples of same-gender couples parenting school-aged children, and so kids in these neighborhoods grow up seeing differences modeled in the family arrangements of their friends. But in other areas, there are very few same-gender couples with school-aged children, and so children in elementary school may not have had the opportunity to interact with persons who come from LGBTQ+ households. Whether there are few LGBTQ parents in the neighborhood or many, it is important that children grow up knowing that there are different ways to be in a family together.

Children may grow up knowing from a very early age whether or not they are attracted to members of the opposite sex, the same sex, or perhaps both. From an early age, children experience their gender identity in ways that match the gender they are assigned at birth because of their sex, or they experience their gender in ways that do not match the gender they were assigned. It is important that parents and teachers know how to support LGBTQ children and youth from a young age, particularly because of the high rates of anxiety and suicide among these youth. Resources like those provided by GLSEN (pronounced "glisten") can help educators provide a safer environment for youth.[9]

The majority of school-aged reading material currently focuses on relationships between men and women, and middle-grade books rarely include characters that are not heterosexual. If there is a love interest or a crush developing in a story, it is exceedingly rare that any romantic affection is expressed between members of the same gender. This perpetuates the image that families only look one way, with men and women as the parents, and it fails to give young people who are already experiencing their first crushes a mirror of a couple that looks like the kind of relationship they would like to have one day.

Carolyn Shares: *Princess Princess Ever After*

A good exception to this rule is the juvenile graphic novel *Princess Princess Ever After* by Katie O'Neill. It is a comic book for middle-grade readers about two princesses, one of whom rescues the other from a tower. Princess Amira, a dark-skinned princess, approaches a tower on her horse with her sword, responding to a scream coming from the top of the tower. She rescues the imprisoned princess from the tower, learning her name is Sadie. As the story continues, Princess Amira discovers that Princess Sadie has been trapped by her evil older sister. Using mean taunts about Sadie being stupid and fat, the older sister has convinced Sadie that she belongs in the tower. Consequently, Sadie had sabotaged previous princes from rescuing her. Yet she allows Amira to rescue her, because seeing Amira makes her want to escape. The two protagonists go on to

---

[9]For numbers and statistics, as well as posters and infographics that parents and teachers can use to raise awareness of the experiences of LGBTQ youth, go to the website for GLSEN's 2017 National School Climate Study: https://www.glsen.org/article/2017-national-school-climate-survey.

face other obstacles, and in the end, as in many fairy tales, they get married. The big differences in this story are that the marriage is between two princesses, and that throughout the story the signs and hints of a love developing between the two young women are clear.

I brought this story to read to my daughter's third-grade class. I read aloud while showing the pictures to the students. At the end, when the two princesses face each other in a wedding scene, a student in the class asked, "Are they getting married?" As soon as I said, "Yes!" another child blurted out, "But they're both girls!" I affirmed the student's observation: "That's right! They are both girls. Do you know any girls who married each other? Or boys who married boys? There are lots of different kinds of families out there, and maybe you know of other kids who have two moms or two dads." Another girl in the class spoke up—a girl who had previously made it known to others that she just had a mom and no dad, only a "sperm donor,"—pointing out that her family was different too: "Yeah, like I don't have a dad."

This conversation opened up new possibilities for these children to see the differences among them, and the possibilities of what families might look like. Perhaps for some students, this was one of the first (if not *the* first) time that they had seen same-gendered attraction demonstrated in literature. Naming differences and showing examples of such difference in a positive light can help normalize the experiences of children who may already be feeling attracted to persons of the same gender and wonder if they are "normal."

Joy Shares: Sexuality Is Happening in School

Parents, let me be the first to help you realize that sexuality happens in schools! Whether your child is *straight* or LBGTQ, the expression and figuring out of who one is happens in school. Think about it. From kindergarten, or perhaps before, most children are in school with teachers and classmates day in and day out for thirteen years. In addition to the parties, the soccer games, the music lessons, and the holiday celebrations, they are also engaging those who are different from them—and some are figuring out that they are the ones who are different.

I will never forget my first year of teaching in New York City public schools. I was a New York City Teaching Fellow, attending class at St. John's University in the evening and teaching during the day. Professor Pedota, now retired, from St. Johns told my cohort every evening we met that teaching in NYC public schools was "trial by fire." To me, teaching at this middle school in Long Island City felt as if I had been dropped in the fiery furnace and the doors had been slammed shut.

One day as I attempted to teach a lesson in math to my eighth-grade class, I realized something was going on. If my memory serves me correctly, the students had come in from lunch and we were settling in to the last half of the day. The issue was between two female students. One student, I could see, was not at all happy. I took her outside. "Jessica, what's wrong?" I asked. It took her a minute to respond. She looked down avoiding my eyes. "Michelle...keeps touching me," she said. Confused, I said, "What do you mean?" "She likes me. And she tries to touch me and get near me, and I don't like her like that."

I was stunned. Like, whoa! I didn't realize this happened in middle school. Part of the reason was that I had not encountered this before—it was a new experience for me. I was getting a huge education in this moment and still had to figure out how to manage it. So I asked Jessica, "Did you tell Michelle that you do not like her touching you?" "Yes," she replied, "but she's not really listening." I said, "Okay, I will talk to her."

I called Michelle out of the room and into the hallway. She leaned up against the wall in a nonchalant way, a manner usually associated with how a boy might carry himself. "What's going on Michelle?" I asked. "Nothing." Realizing that perhaps she was not going to offer much in the way of conversation, I cut to the heart of the matter. "Look. Jessica is pretty and you like her. I get it. But you can't put your hands on her because you like her. You have to respect her space and her wishes to be left alone." I then went deeper: "You know there's a lot going on here and you don't need any trouble. It's your last year. Graduation is coming soon. It's okay to like her and find her attractive, but you have to exercise some self-control. If she does not want you to touch her—then you can't." Michelle nodded that she understood.

Truthfully, I was nervous. And in hindsight I don't understand why, except for the fact that it was two young women. If this had been a boy and a girl, it would have been a typical situation, maybe even one that was dismissed or ignored—or more specifically a situation familiar to me. These two young women educated me that day. I learned that sexuality is happening in middle school, and probably younger, and that I should not put my head in the sand.

I was also proud of myself. I did not condemn Michelle for being attracted to another girl. Why would I? Well, most of us for better or for worse have a particular framework that we have been taught. I acknowledge that I have been unlearning some of that over my lifetime. I also realize that as a teacher in that moment, what was most important was that each child felt understood and respected as I attempted to settle an issue. I hope that Jessica knew that I understood her desire not to be touched. I served as a mediator to help communicate that message to Michelle. I hope that Michelle also knew that I understood that she was attracted to Jessica and that she wanted to express that attraction. However, Michelle also needed to know that it was important to respect another person's wishes to not be touched. Whew! Needless to say, this moment is etched in my mind. I was not a parent then, but as a parent now I am more attuned to the ways in which children and adolescents explore and express their sexuality.

Joy Shares: Teaching the Teacher

I've been teaching professionally since 2004. I've taught sixth grade through graduate school. Each age group has its positives and challenges. I still enjoy going into the schools and helping children, although the public schools can often feel like a battleground. Not that higher education is always a peach; whether undergraduate or graduate, many students have a sense of entitlement, and some will talk back and will take it out on your evaluation too. Yet I *love* teaching! And as much as I try to teach and impart something of value to the students who come across my path, they always seem to teach me something too.

One fall a couple of years ago, I did my part by welcoming students into my class and then, of course, in teacherly fashion called the roll. It was an innocent enough task. Well, I got to one name and it was one generally considered to be a female name. I read it aloud, "Amy Betram?" (name changed). However, the student responded with a different name, one generally associated with a male. "Actually, no, it is Robert Betram. They have not changed it yet in the Registrar's office." Huh? I was confused. I mean she, actually *he*, did not look like an Amy, but the voice and the build of the body could have been either. I was still clueless in the moment, which felt like a really long time—like standing on stage and forgetting your lines. And then the light bulb went off. Ohhhhhhhhhh! I get it now. The student was transgender. "Okay. No problem," I said, and continued calling the class roll. I had heard of people being transgender before but, at least to my knowledge, I had not met anyone who *was* transgender. After class, the student came to me and continued to explain the mix-up—not that he needed to. I apologized because I honestly had not known. I had called the name on the page, but while the mistake, whoever it was, may or may not have embarrassed Robert, it certainly taught me a thing or two.

I learned that I love teaching. It never mattered to me that Amy was now Robert. I was honestly surprised, but then again who wouldn't be? I had to do a quick paradigm shift—and it was definitely a teachable moment! What I did care about was that Robert was a student in my class and I had a responsibility to Robert to impart the same knowledge that I would try to impart to all of the other students, to care for him as I cared for all my students.

The lesson to be learned here, dear reader, is an old cliché: Never judge a book by its cover; you may end up missing out on a great book.

Chapter 4 Activity for Self-Reflection

Gender and Sexuality

Does talking about gender identity or sexual orientation make you feel *afraid*? Perhaps a better "A" word would be "awkward"? Do you want to *back away* from this conversation? Or try to *control* the terms of the debate? Notice your own automatic responses and write them down.

Taking a deep breath, return to these responses and *acknowledge* your feelings. *Be present* to whatever you are feeling. *Come closer* and keep going.

Access other sources of information to help you learn more about issues of gender or sexual orientation that give you pause. There are lists of books among the Appendices, some of which can help you talk about gender and sexual orientation with young people, and some that can help you be more informed as an adult. *Build* relationships with persons who may have a different take on this than you do, and *cultivate* an openness to learning more from others.

5

Relearning Race

Just as we are becoming more aware of the differences and commonalities between people previously marked as distinctly "male" and "female," so too we are continuing to relearn the concept of "race." Depending on where you grew up and when, you may have learned about race starting from an early age, or you may have experienced grown-ups avoiding the topic as much as possible. Like gender, race is also a category label that keeps changing, and it is important that we know its history and impact.

Race is another identity that is both received from society and formed internally by how we respond to it. What society sees on the outside does not always match how the person feels about him or herself on the inside. Race is a social construct, which means that the way in which people are categorized into "races" has changed over time, depending upon the rules of society.

Historical events affect social "common sense" about race. For example, persons who were from places in the Middle East may have been considered "white" before September 11, 2001, but since then they have been scapegoated, disrespected, and called by blanket terms such as Arabs or Muslims.[1] In the early twentieth century, persons who had immigrated from Ireland or Italy were identified by their ethnicity as distinctly "not-white," but these groups eventually became more associated with "whiteness" and have benefited from that designation.[2]

---

[1]Kumarini Silva, *Brown Threat: Identification in the Security State* (Minneapolis: University of Minnesota Press, 2016).

[2]David Roediger, *Working Toward Whiteness: How America's Immigrants Became White* (New York: Basic Book, 2005).

Think of your own background: Do you know where your parents came from? From which countries of origin did your ancestors emigrate in order to live where they live now? Were your ancestors among the millions taken by force from their homeland to work here enslaved? Or were they among the indigenous peoples living on this land before the Spanish "discovered" it and Europeans colonized it? Perhaps your ancestors came here as laborers to work during the California Gold Rush in the 1800s, only to have Congress pass the Chinese Exclusion Act of 1882 to deny citizenship to persons from China.

Were your ancestors granted citizenship as "naturalized" white people for as long as they lived here? Or did they have to fight the Supreme Court (as Takao Ozawa did in 1922 or Bhagat Singh Thind did in 1923) for citizenship on the basis of looking "white," only to have their petitions denied, with the United States's highest court ruling they were *racially* ineligible for naturalization as citizens? Were there any challenges with being associated with your race or ethnicity in distant or recent family memory?

What about now—do you currently experience bias because of your race or ethnicity? Do you have any stories from family members about how "things have changed" over time? In other words, were they treated differently than you are today? How different groups are treated in society changes over time, with some groups remaining at the top and others shifting in position relative to other people groups.

What does this have to do with our young children? They have been born into a racialized society. They will be seen as part of a particular "race" whether or not you raise them to be conscious of that race. The question of racial identity development enters in when thinking about how you want your child to relate to that racialization. How do you want your child to think about being categorized as a member of the "race" of which others see her or him? How do you want your child to feel? Note that the answers to these questions typically depend on whether your child is racialized into a group with greater or less status and privilege.

For instance, despite the fact that the category "white" covers a broad range of ethnicities and experiences, many scholars have pointed out the relative status and advantages whites have in society compared to people of color. These advantages can be seen in historical policies that gave whites full rights to citizenship and property while denying these same rights to people of color. Zoning practices and racial segregation of housing and schools continue to have an impact on communities of color, whereas it is easier for white children to gain access to higher-rated schools, more resources, better jobs, and mortgages in "better" neighborhoods. So, if your child is regarded as "white" and is born into these advantages that probably appear "natural" to you, how can you keep him or her from internalizing false messages of superiority over others?

If your child is regarded as a "person of color," or more specifically as someone who is African American, Latinx, or Asian American, early on they may be exposed to messages that suggest that they are inferior to their white classmates. Children of color may feel insecure or left out, or even be identified more often as the "trouble-makers" in class. For this reason, they need to be supported in seeing themselves positively and in being able to affirm their own self-worth when society sends them contrary messages.

Children of color who are in schools with kids who mostly look like them, schools that are underfunded and under-resourced, may compare themselves to the white kids across town who have access to the latest technologies and better facilities. When children make these comparisons, they often wonder why it is that people who look white get things that people of color don't. As we saw in the study of preschoolers asked to choose which adult they preferred— the one who was treated well or the one treated poorly—they may begin to prefer people who are white simply because they are treated better than people of color.[3]

---

[3]Allison Skinner, Andrew N. Meltzoff, and Kristina R. Olson, "'Catching' Social Bias: Exposure to Biased Nonverbal Signals Creates Social Biases in Preschool Children," *Psychological Science* 28, no. 2 (2017): 216–224. Available online: https://www.researchgate.net/profile/Andrew_Meltzoff/publication/316630264_ Catching_social_bias_Exposure_to_biased_nonverbal_signals_creates_social_biases _in_preschool_children/links/5908ad10a6fdcc496163e74d/Catching-social-bias-Exposure-to-biased-nonverbal-signals-creates-social-biases-in-preschool-children.pdf. Cited in Jennifer Eberhardt, *Biased*, 35.

How can you help children avoid internalizing these messages?

Psychologist Beverly Daniel Tatum has written about stages of racial identity development, both for whites and for people of color. Because the messages society sends to these two broad categories of people are different, how we hope to shape children's response to these messages also needs to differ.

White children may feel a sense of superiority over classmates of color, even if that feeling is subconscious, simply because of the messages they receive from society. Therefore, white children need to be able to see how society can be unfair in making things easier for them and harder for others. By becoming aware of this unfairness, they can speak out against it when they see it in their classrooms and peer groups.

Carolyn Shares: "Mom, Are We White?"

When my daughter was three, we were celebrating Martin Luther King Jr. Day, and I was trying to explain to her why he is held in such high esteem. In simple language, I told her that many white people were being mean to black people, and he stood up for black people and made white people treat them better. My blond-haired, blue-eyed daughter looked at me with wide eyes, and asked me, "Mom, are *we* white?" The question came from a place of concern: Here were people who looked like her mom and dad being the "bad guys" in history, and this made her worried. Already, she had a sense of right and wrong and knew that treating people badly was wrong. Did that mean that she and her parents were also bad?

In response, I brought up a picture online of the March on Washington, and I zoomed in on the crowd of people who had come to gather and listen to Dr. King speak. Up close, she could see the faces of the people in attendance—many were black, but some were white. I pointed out to her that there were white people who were working to make other white people treat black people better, and she could see some of them in the picture.

One of the stages of racial identity development theory for children involves giving them role models of people who look like them who are doing the good work we hope they will want to do someday. The importance of role models is echoed again and again in the field of education, where advocates urge teachers to include pictures of a diversity of people and families so that children can see themselves reflected in the role models we are holding up for them. Both white children and children of color need to see people who look like them living into the values we hope they will embody.

Shame and Silence around Differences

As children learn the language of difference, teachers and parents can inadvertently teach them that differences are bad. If a child with light skin points out another child's dark skin, the nearest adult may try to "shush" the child into not calling attention to race. This sends a message to the child: Skin color is not something we can talk about without getting into trouble. Enough of these kinds of encounters sends the message to the child that skin color, and the associations between skin color and race, are important to avoid mentioning and that they carry a stigma or embarrassment. The sense of embarrassment gets communicated from a parent or teacher who does not feel comfortable talking about race; by being "shushed," the child then feels embarrassed for having brought up the topic.

Children from different racial and ethnic backgrounds need to be able to use language that is appropriate for talking about other people that does not devalue or make strange the differences of others. By naming the ways children come from different families, parents can point out that children may have the same color of skin or have different skin tones. Encourage children to ask questions about their own parents' family history. Rather than asking people where they are "from" (which typically gets asked of persons who are not white), children can begin to learn about the traditions and differences among their own friends and relatives.

This requires more than just celebrating differences, however. It also means helping children through books and group conversations to recognize how we use stereotypes in ways that hurt the feelings of our peers. We need to give children the language of unfairness related to biases against certain groups of people. Naming bias in a way that children can understand can happen through a variety of helpful activities and books. At the end of this book, you will find resources to help you talk to children about these differences.

Carolyn Shares: "She Just Said 'Brown Skin'!"

Some children grow up in households where race is a frequent topic of discussion. In others, however, race is never mentioned. Young people whose parents have not educated them on the history of racism may find it challenging to talk about it.

Two white third-grade girls were over at my house watching the movie *Home*. The main character of the movie is named Tip, who lives in New York with her mom; they are from Barbados. Tip becomes separated from her mother when aliens colonize the earth and relocate all humans onto a single continent. At one point in the film, you see Tip's mom trying to find her daughter, and she tells someone else what her daughter looks like, saying, "She's got beautiful brown skin and brown hair; *please*, you have to help me!"

One of my daughter's nine-year-old friends was watching the movie with us and said aloud, "She just said 'brown skin'! That's racist. She shouldn't say that."

I tried to intervene. "Actually, she's just stating the fact that her daughter's skin is brown. And that her brown skin is beautiful. People come in all shades and colors, and they're all beautiful." The girls did not say anything in response.

This nine-year-old child had learned (either at home or school or through media portrayals) that it was not okay to talk about the color of someone's skin. Some people believe that racism means noticing race, and that to avoid being racist, we must not notice or draw attention to race. The sayings "I don't see color" or "I'm colorblind" come from this notion that racism is labeling people into different races.

However, children *do* recognize skin color, and only a small percentage of the population are actually "colorblind," which means they cannot distinguish between certain colors (usually red and green). Such people can still be racist, even if they are physically "colorblind."

Racism has less to do with the words we use to talk about skin color and more to do with the story we tell ourselves about people of different skin colors. Racism involves the history of policies and practices that have made it harder for people of color to enjoy full rights as citizens, as well as the story we tell ourselves about why there is inequality—a story that typically blames people of color. Racism is about the stereotypes that lead people to see people of color as "threats." Consider situations where law enforcement has reacted with lethal force against people of color, and compare them to incidents where white men have committed mass shootings and been taken alive.

For children to develop consciously into *anti*-racists, they need to be *racism-aware*. This means being familiar with the history of race in this country, and knowing that race is not biology but a way that people have grouped others together based on certain physical characteristics. Youth need to know that race does not mean we are different from one another on the inside, but that we may have different experiences from one another because of racism.

Racial Identity for Adolescents

If your children are white, you may or may not have raised them to be conscious of their whiteness. You may have worried that naming their whiteness would turn them into white supremacists. But you do not have to emphasize whiteness as a trait of superiority in order to name it; in fact, it is important that you name the subtle messages of white supremacy so that your children can be critical of that message.

Psychologists who have studied racial identity development emphasize how important it is that both children of color and white children are able to recognize the impact of race in society and to cultivate a *positive anti-racist* identity.[4] For white children, this means unlearning subconscious patterns of viewing themselves as superior to people of color. For children of color, it means helping them

---

[4]Janet Helms, *Black and White Racial Identity: Theory, Research, and Practice* (New York: Greenwood Press, 1990); Beverly Daniel Tatum, "Talking about Race, Learning about Racism: 'The Application of' Racial Identity Development Theory in the Classroom," *Harvard Educational Review* 62, no.1 (1992).

identify the harmful messages and stereotypes that society sends them, so they do not internalize these messages unknowingly. In addition to unlearning racism, children need to learn how to work actively against racism. Unlearning racism and working against racism means being able to identify what racism looks like and what impact it has on individuals and society.

The Health Impact of Racism on Children of Color

The American Academy of Pediatrics in 2019 published a document on "The Impact of Racism on Child and Adolescent Health."[5] The Academy defines racism as a "system of structuring opportunity and assigning value based on the social interpretation of how one looks (which is what we call 'race') that unfairly disadvantages some individuals and communities, unfairly advantages other individuals and communities, and saps the strength of the whole society through the waste of human resources."[6] The doctors who conducted this research reported that racism affects children before they are even born, such as in the higher rates of maternal deaths for black, Hispanic, and American Indian women compared to white women.[7] Throughout a child's development, racism plays out institutionally (where the child is able to live and go to school), interpersonally (whether the child's teacher has low expectations of achievement for children of color, for example), and internally (as the child fears living into stereotypes about not succeeding as a person of color, and self-doubt and despair if she or he does confirm stereotypes).[8]

---

[5]Maria Trent, Danielle G. Dooley, and Jacqueline Dougé, AAP Section on Adolescent Health, AAP Council on Community Pediatrics, AAP Committee on Adolescence, "The Impact of Racism on Child and Adolescent Health," *Pediatrics,* 144, no. 2 (August 2019), https://pediatrics.aappublications.org/content/144/2/e20191765.

[6]Citing Camara Phyllis Jones, Benedict I. Truman, Laurie D. Elam-Evans, et al., "Using 'Socially Assigned Race' to Probe White Advantages in Health Status," *Ethnicity & Disease* 18, no. 4 (Autumn 2008): 495–504.

[7]Roni Caryn Rabin, "Huge Racial Disparities Found in Deaths Linked to Pregnancy," *The New York Times,* May 7, 2019, https://www.nytimes.com/2019/05/07/health/pregnancy-deaths-.html?searchResultPosition=1&module=inline.

[8]Perri Klass, "The Impact of Racism on Children's Health," *The New York Times,* August 12, 2019, https://www.nytimes.com/2019/08/12/well/family/the-impact-of-racism-on-childrens-health.html.

In his book on stereotyping, Claude Steele writes about the experience of a person who *fears being stereotyped* as its own source of stress—whether or not the person is actually being stereotyped.[9] For instance, the title of his book, *Whistling Vivaldi*, comes from the account of a young black man who has taken to whistling a classical music piece by the composer Vivaldi whenever he is walking near a white person at night or getting on an elevator with a white person. The reason behind this musical interlude is that the young man, being black, has had so many experiences of people assuming he is dangerous that he intentionally tries to counteract that stereotype by putting the other person at ease. By whistling a song by a white classical composer, the man hopes that the white people he encounters will interrupt their association of black men with criminality and instead see him as a person who appreciates classical music and therefore is less of a threat to them.

It is distressing to think about the mental gymnastics this young man has had to endure to come up with this strategy. Claude Steele labels it "stereotype threat," or the fear that one is going to be stereotyped and worrying about how one's actions can challenge or confirm that stereotype. This mental work adds stress to a person's life: Will my actions be perceived as confirming the stereotypes people have about me because of my identity?

"The Talk"

Tragically, this kind of calculation is necessary for some people who fear that their actions, if conforming to a stereotype, may actually lead to their death. Parents of black boys, as well as black girls, report having "the talk" with their children. Not about sex or drugs, but about what to do if a police officer pulls him or her over.

This is not to say that all police officers are bad. This is not to disrespect the men and women who put their lives on the line to serve in law enforcement. But as recent videos have made more apparent to the general public, there are police officers who have responded to black and brown men and women with greater

---

[9]Claude Steele, *Whistling Vivaldi: How Stereotypes Affect Us and What We Can Do* (New York: W.W. Norton, 2010).

force—at times *lethal* force—than would be the case if the person of interest were white.

In a January 2017 episode of the TV show *Grey's Anatomy*, the chief of surgery, Miranda Bailey, has to give her son Tuck "the talk."[10] In the episode, a teenager is brought into the emergency room after having been shot by the police. His crime? Climbing into his bedroom window after he had locked himself out of his house. The episode came out shortly after several similar situations had happened in real life, and the show gave viewers a chance to think about what it might feel like for parents to have this happen to their own child. "The talk" that Dr. Bailey and her husband give their son instructs him to put his hands up in the air, and yell "Don't shoot!" and then in a calm and steady voice to tell the police his name, his age, and that he is not armed.[11]

He is not to raise his voice. He is not to reach for his cell phone. He is not to talk back to the police. He is not to run. None of these actions is a crime, but given how many black men and women police have shot—even shot dead—for such innocent actions, it is understandable that parents of boys and girls of color prepare their children for the real danger they can face every day.

Adolescent Identity Projects

At this age, children may already have developed some sort of "identity project," or a way of understanding who they are and how they are unique from others. Scholars have described "identity projects" as "a source of meaning that provides a sense of self and is linked to concrete activities to which youth commit themselves."[12] Adolescents are looking for ways to define themselves, and if they can have something with which to identify, whether it be a sport or a hobby or another interest, they may develop a sense of self around that interest.

---

[10]*Grey's Anatomy*, season 14, episode 10, "Personal Jesus," directed by Kevin Rodney Sullivan, written by Zoanne Clack, aired January 25, 2018 on ABC.

[11]Lesley Goldberg, "Why 'Grey's Anatomy' Just Overtly Tackled Unconscious Bias," *The Hollywood Reporter*, January 25, 2018, https://www.hollywoodreporter.com/live-feed/why-greys-anatomy-just-overtly-tackled-unconscious-bias-1078509.

[12]Stephanie Deluca, Susan Clampet-Lundquist, and Kathryn Edin, *Coming of Age in the Other America* (New York: Russell Sage Foundation, 2016), 66.

Books aimed at adolescents demonstrate this well. In the juvenile novel *The Epic Fail of Arturo Zamora,* the main character is a thirteen-year-old Cuban American boy who is faced with losing his grandmother, losing his family's restaurant to a greedy developer, and messing up a relationship with a girl he likes.[13] In the course of the book, he discovers the poetry of José Martí, a Cuban patriot who died fighting for independence from Spain in the nineteenth century. Through the poetry of Martí, young Arturo Zamora is able to connect his identity more securely to his Cuban immigrant grandparents and find in their story and Martí's the courage he needs to fight for what he loves. The novel shows us how "identity projects," or the ways that young people can find their identity in the examples set for them by others, can empower and guide youth as they make their way in the world.

As kids learn more about racial dynamics in society, helping them associate with positive examples of people who look like them and are doing good in the world can help them formulate an identity that is positive and help them make sense of the world. If your child is white, it might be helpful to lift up figures within their field of interest who are engaged in practices of community and embracing diversity. Help them know that there are other white people out there who are working against racism and the unfair benefits white people have received over time. By seeing other white people who have challenged the message of white supremacy, they can see how they, too, can make a difference for good.

If you have a child of color, it is important that they, too, have role models who look like them. Whether your heritage is Native Hawaiian, Filipino, Mexican, Nigerian, Pakistani, Chinese, Indian, Korean, Caribbean, or Native American, or any other nationality, it is important that they have role models who reflect the kind of people they want to grow up to be. It is also important for youth of color to connect with a history of struggle and perseverance, learning how their ancestors have worked to build community and make their way in the world.

---

[13]Pablo Cartaya, *The Epic Fail of Arturo Zamora* (New York: Viking, 2017).

Carolyn Shares: Third Culture Kids

A group of women is meeting in a side room at a local coffee shop. If you were to look in from the window and see them, you might not consider the group "diverse." They are all white or white-appearing, they are about the same age, and they all have school-aged children. They look like they fit right in among their neighbors in this predominantly white suburb of Austin. And yet as you hear them talk, you learn about the isolation they feel as immigrants.

All of these white women have come from somewhere other than the United States. One comes from South Africa, another from Australia, still another from Spain, another from France, and another from the Philippines. Two more women sit down and join them; one is from China, another from India.

This group of women has come together to talk about a book called *Third Culture Kids: Growing Up Among Worlds,* by Ruth Van Reken and Michael Pollack.[14] The book explains the experiences of persons who grow up in a country different from the one that is considered their "home" country, for example because their parents are missionaries or government officials or employees of an international corporation. Generally, such persons are known as "expatriates," or "ex-pats," and persons who grow up in this environment often share some similarities, particularly when it comes to the challenges of returning to the country considered their "home" country. The label "third culture kids" comes from the fact that children growing up in a country different from the one in which they will eventually reside as adults often feel out of place: They do not feel they fit in with the culture of their host country, but when they return to their home country, they also feel disconnected. This "third culture," of having lived between worlds, is a cultural experience that persons share with others who have grown up overseas or in international contexts.

Some of the mothers in the group want to learn more about the concept of "third culture kids," to understand not only their own experience as immigrants but also that of their children. Several

---

[14]David C. Pollack, Ruth E. Van Reken and Michael V. Pollack, *Third Culture Kids: Growing Up Among Worlds, 3d ed.* (Boston: Nicholas Brealey, 2017).

of them have children who were born in the United States, then lived internationally before resettling in the U.S. for the second half of their children's adolescence. Still others immigrated when their children were still quite young, but they noticed a difference in their children when they periodically returned to visit family in the country in which the parents grew up. The children felt different from the children in their school, but they also did not seem to fit in with the children of the culture of their parents.

My (Carolyn) husband Phil grew up in Thailand for the first ten years of his life. He has shared with me his awkward experiences of returning to live in Indiana when his parents moved back to the United States. He felt a sense of isolation from his peers because none of them could ask about his background or life in Thailand; these ten-year-olds living in a depressed town in the Midwest had no context for understanding his life across the ocean in an entirely different culture. And yet knowing other cultures and having these rich experiences as a kid has made him much more comfortable interacting with people from many different backgrounds. He is more open to the ideas of others, because he has seen how much our ideas are shaped by where we grow up.

Experiencing the richness of other ethnicities and cultures can really expand a person's horizons. Although it is challenging to feel like an outsider at times in other cultures, it helps us see things in new ways. We can see possibilities in the world where before we had been limited by our point of view.

Being more comfortable in multiple cultural contexts can also make us more adept at building cross-cultural relationships. A woman originally from France shared with me the following story. Her nine-year-old daughter came home one day saying the other children told her she wasn't really American. Her mother reassured her, saying that she was indeed American because she had been born in the United States. But the other children had insisted that the girl wasn't really American because her parents were not from America. The mom reflected that the experience may have influenced her daughter's subsequent choice of friends; over the years since that experience her closest friends have been children whose parents also came from outside the U.S.

If our children can be friends just as easily with persons whose parents come from China, Pakistan, India, and Mexico, then they are already learning skills that will be essential for the social community they have inherited.

Multiracial Identity and Diversity

Spending time with people who have lived in other countries can remind us that "race" is a very historical and contextual concept, and as those contexts change in a global society, so too do our ideas about race. People who are "white" in America may be religious or ethnic minorities in the country from which they come. Children of parents from different races or ethnic backgrounds may not identify with one race or culture over another. They are part of a growing generation of "multiracials"—people who identify as part of both of their parents' ancestry.

In *The New Face of America: How the Emerging Multiracial, Multiethnic Majority Is Changing the United States*, author Eric Bailey names how frequently multiracials are overlooked in the race conversation.[15] Interviewing young people who identify as multiracial, Bailey hears over and over again the struggle these young people have with claiming an identity. Being multiracial can pit a child against their parents: Are they more like one parent (and that parent's race) or the other? If one parent is black, the child may struggle with being "black enough," or "white enough" if one parent is white, when hanging out with peers who are not multiracial.

Thomas Chatterton Williams, a writer for the *New York Times Magazine*, published *Self-Portrait in Black and White: Unlearning Race*, a book that shares his own experience as a light-skinned man born to a black father and white mother.[16] His children, both with blond hair and blue eyes, make him question the categories of black and

---

[15]Eric Bailey, *The New Face of America: How the Emerging Multiracial, Multiethnic Majority Is Changing the United States* (Santa Barbara, Calif.: Praeger, 2013).

[16]Thomas Chatterton Williams, *Self-Portrait in Black and White: Unlearning Race* (New York: W.W. Norton, 2019).

white and reflect on the troubled history of racial identity. It was important for his own father that Williams identify as black. Yet when his first daughter was born, he found himself trying to change the filters on his camera when he sent pictures out to friends and family after her birth; he tried to hide the fact that she appeared white.

Television shows are highlighting more of these experiences, too. The ABC television show *Mixed-ish* focuses on the experience of growing up biracial in the 1980s. The show follows the young Rainbow "Bow" Johnson, whose mother is black and father is white, as she adjusts to life after her family leaves a hippie commune. Because of the dramatic change from the context of a supposedly colorblind commune to a public school, Bow and her siblings have to choose whether to sit at the black kids' table or the white kids' table during school lunch. Does Bow identify more with her mom or her dad? This causes a lot of stress until she decides she can choose both: She finds a friend who will sit with her at a table in the middle.

The show's third episode, "Let Your Hair Down," explores the complicated relationship between hair and race and celebrates the beauty of natural black hair.[17] Bow is told by her white teacher to wear her hair "neat" for picture day, which prompts a family discussion about white standards of beauty and about expectations that black women spend hours using chemicals on their hair to straighten it. The narrator, actress, and show producer, Tracee Ellis Ross, remarks that "good hair" may sound like a compliment, but because it represents the standards of white beauty (straight hair), it has never been good for black self-esteem. The show ends with a present-day celebration: the announcement that the State of California had passed the first law preventing employers from discriminating against natural hair. The "CROWN Act" (Create a Respectful and Open Workplace for Natural Hair) was signed into law on July 3, 2019, by California Governor Gavin Newsom.[18]

---

[17]*Mixed-Ish*, season 1, episode 3, "Let Your Hair Down," directed by Michael Spiller, written by Karin Gist and Peter Saji, aired October 8, 2019, on ABC.

[18]The full text of California State Senate Bill 188 can be found online: https://leginfo.legislature.ca.gov/faces/billTextClient.xhtml?bill_id=201920200SB188.

Naming Racial Difference in Order to Name Discrimination

The word "discrimination" refers to treating people differently based on particular characteristics. It is a legal term, used to describe unlawful actions of treating one person differently than another based on certain categories such as race or gender or age.

By naming race, it is not our intention to recalcify old terms or ways of thinking. Instead, it is important to name race because of the ways people of color continue to be treated differently than white-appearing people. For instance, in today's society, whiteness continues to provide white children a buffer of assumed privilege. White youth are less likely to be seen as dangerous or suspicious, and white teens are less likely to be convicted for drug-related offenses, even though their use of drugs is statistically equal to that of other populations.

This is not to minimize the challenges that white kids experience—different aspects of our identity lead to being treating differently by society—and white kids may sometimes have other identities that make them a target of bullying or other struggles. Third culture kids who are white-appearing and yet feel like they don't fully belong have their own struggles and stresses. And yet on a societal level, third culture kids who appear white will continue to benefit from a system that racializes them as white. To say that they experience feelings of isolation in this culture does not necessarily translate to their being aware of or empathetic towards persons whom this society sees as perpetual outsiders because of the color of their skin.

One way we can respond to this is to continue to talk about issues of difference and ways people can make changes in society. Return to the ABCs, remembering our automatic responses, practicing more intentional personal reflection, and then looking for ways you can employ the interpersonal ABCs to try and make a difference where you can.

Teaching all children about the unfairness that has been part of our history, including the ways white people and white children have been given unfair advantages, can help children speak out when they notice unfair treatment—toward themselves or others. We need all children to learn about our history and the ongoing ways that our society makes things unfair and harder for some than for others, so that all of our kids have a greater opportunity to thrive and live into who they are.

Chapter 5 Activity for Self-Reflection

What Do I Believe?

How do you describe your own race? When did you first learn about your race? How have your views about race changed over time?

Name a group about whom you were taught something negative. Who taught you or said negative things to you about this group? How do you feel about this person who said negative things to you about this group? How do you feel *now* about the group of persons about whom you were taught negative things? Are you a friend of anyone in this group? Why? Why not?

Allow yourself some time to sit with the ABCs of diversity regarding race. Listen to your own tendency to be *afraid* to talk about this difficult subject. Look for instances when you might have wanted to *back away* from this conversation, or to *control* the topic so it could be changed. Then spend time *acknowledging* the difficulty of this conversation, and *be present* to the feelings that it brings up. Find ways to *come closer* to this subject, learning more through podcasts and books.

Think about the ways your own race has impacted your *access* to people, places, or other resources. Have you ever been denied entry into a space because of your race? Have you ever felt ignored or treated more rudely because of your race? Or has your race enabled you to gain access into any of the places you want to go? Take a moment to acknowledge once again any feelings that come up for you in these reflections and be present to them.

Find ways to *build* relationships with persons from different races from yourself and to *cultivate* conversations about how race continues to impact people in your community. As uncomfortable as it may feel, it is important to raise awareness of the ongoing and everyday ways implicit bias affects people's daily lives.

In cultivating an openness to hard conversations about racism, remember to take care of yourself. Talking about painful subjects can bring a lot of feelings to the surface, and in order to build on our relationships together, we need to deepen our capacity to tend to our own feelings so we can be present to the feelings of others.

6

Fears of Fitting Out: Religious Differences

In the 2014 movie *Home*, the alien character named Oh admits to his human friend that he does not fit in with his other aliens, that instead he "fits out." The reason his name is Oh is because that is the sound the other aliens make when he gets close to them—the sound of disappointment. This "fitting out" is a painful experience for Oh, though he tries to pretend he does not notice it.[1]

When children go through elementary school, they seek to fit in and find approval among their peers. While children may have their own interests and style in clothes, they are also aware of what other children are interested in and what clothes they see other children wearing. Because they pay attention to pop culture references and other colloquial idioms, children will inevitably come home saying things they heard from their peers.

Children vary in how comfortable they feel expressing their own difference. They also vary in how easily they admit they are different in some way from the rest of the class. If children point out differences in others, it is often to tease the one who is different.

As children grow from being unselfconscious toddlers to school-aged children and eventually adolescents, there seems to be a greater risk involved in sticking out from the crowd. Kids typically don't want to be different. They do not want to stand out. It can feel really vulnerable to share ways that you might be different, because

---

[1]*Home,* directed by Tim Johnson (USA, DreamWorks Animation, 2015).

(with good reason!) kids worry about their friends shunning them for being too "weird."

Carolyn Shares: "One Thing Nobody Knows about You"

The second-grade Girl Scouts had gathered for their first campout, sleeping in tents under the starry skies in the safety of one of the girls' backyards. As they sat around a fire pit roasting marshmallows, the seven- and eight-year-old girls were losing focus—some girls wanted to wander off, others had no intention of eating enflamed marshmallows, and one had gotten her feelings hurt already by being passed over in the line to use the metal roasting skewers. It was a bit of a mess.

I tried to gather us all together by posing a question: "What's one thing you think no one here knows about you?"

The girls got quiet, and then one by one they began to offer up pieces of their hidden lives to the group:

"I'm afraid of the dark."

"I'm afraid of snakes."

"Some of you already know this about me, but I am not a sweets person—I don't like chocolate!"

"What?! No way! I *love* chocolate! But what I don't like is popcorn."

"I got to see Taylor Swift in concert."

"One thing nobody knows about me is that I'm Ismaili."

"Smiley!? What? I'm smiley, too!" (Several girls erupted into laughter.)

"I'm afraid of dogs."

The girls kept going around in a circle, but the one who had said she was Ismaili was taken aback by the laughter. I saw her draw away from the circle, turn her face, and look away as the rest of the girls kept going around, naming what they thought no one knew about them.

Later that night, as the girls were in their sleeping bags in tents, I overheard her talking with two of the other girls who shared a tent with her.

"This was the worst night of my life."

"What?! Oh no! Why?!" Her friends seemed really surprised.

"Everybody laughed at me when I said I was Ismaili."

"I didn't even hear what you said!"

"Yeah, I didn't hear you. I didn't laugh at you."

"We didn't laugh at you—I'm sorry."

Her friends' words seemed to cheer her some, and they continued to talk in hushed tones until I and the other adults began reinforcing the "no talking!" rule.

But what really stuck with me was the sense of vulnerability it took for this girl to share with her friends her religious identity. It was because none of the others was familiar with the word *Ismaili,* which is a sect within the Shia branch of Islam, that none of them was able to make sense of the word when she used it.

It felt very brave for this seven- or eight-year-old to share her faith, not only because it was a tradition unfamiliar to her peers but also because of the political atmosphere. This was the fall of 2017, not even a year after President Donald Trump initiated travel bans for persons wishing to come to the U.S. from majority-Muslim countries. This ban sent the message that Muslims should be kept out of this country, and along with comments Trump had made during his election campaign, it seemed to add fuel to the fire of white nationalists' perpetuating anti-Muslim hate crimes.[2]

As an adult watching the scenario take place, I was not sure how to respond. I was glad that later other girls in her tent tried to make her feel comfortable, but I wondered how she would feel about sharing her faith with other friends in the future. My daughter is among this girl's friends, and when I reminded my daughter of this incident, she told me that her friend has never spoken about her religion since that time.

While we were on the subject, I asked my daughter to comment on the scenario as I had written it, double-checking to make sure it accurately represented what she remembered from that event. She asked if she could "help me write" about this, and she typed the

---

[2]Heidi Beirich, "Trump's Anti-Muslim Words and Policies Have Consequences," *Southern Poverty Law Center,* April 24, 2018, https://www.splcenter.org/news/2018/04/24/trumps-anti-muslim-words-and-policies-have-consequences.

following reflections, which I only edited by adding punctuation and capitalization:

> *What I think is most important about this story is that it shows more about the little things that could possibly be perceived as offensive that most people don't notice but might end up being game-changers for the offended, and in this case the girl made herself vulnerable by letting down her guard and telling this big group of other girls what religion or beliefs she had. Now put yourself in her shoes. Imagine what it would be like to have told a group of say, Buddhists that you were actually Christian, the first thing that came to mind would probably be the worst-case scenarios. For example, you had developed strong bonds with these people and you thought that they might sever those bonds because you didn't believe in the Buddha.*

At the time she was writing this, it was after her bedtime, and I assumed she was offering to write for me as a stalling tactic (she often gets to writing late at night, and I worry it is an excuse not to go to bed on time). But the next day, looking over her writing, I decided to keep it in the text. I was proud of how she was able to write with such empathy, able to put the situation into terms that were relatable for her.

As someone growing up in a Christian family, with two parents who are ordained Presbyterian ministers teaching in a seminary, she has definitely grown up steeped in a particular faith tradition. But she was able to sense the vulnerability of sharing something about your faith—not only because of big political contexts, but because of the immediate context of worrying whether you would "sever those bonds" you had developed with a particular group.

Recently, my daughter slept over at this girl's house, and I mentioned the incident to her mother. We were sitting in their living room, opposite a wall where a large framed picture held an image of a man I did not recognize. I asked her who it was, and she explained that it was the Aga Khan.[3] She explained that as Ismaili

---

[3]"His Highness the Aga Khan," *the.Ismaili,* https://the.ismaili/his-highness-aga-khan.

Muslims, they believe that the Aga Khan is the living descendant of the Prophet Muhammad. She suggested I do some research on him, telling me that the Aga Khan is really into pluralism, inclusivity, and diversity.

Later that weekend, I went to Wikipedia and learned more about Ismailism, reading about its centuries-old history about which I knew nothing, and I found other articles that helped me understand more about the emphasis on pluralism she had mentioned.[4] In particular, a professor Ali Asani wrote about the passages in the Qur'an that emphasize tolerance, and he referenced the work of other Muslim scholars that say the same.[5] Ismaili Muslims are part of the Shia branch of Islam and number more than 20 million adherents, making them a little more than 1 percent of the total population of Muslims around the world.[6] Their beliefs celebrate values of inclusivity, pluralism, and volunteerism. When the Austin-area Ismaili Center or Jamatkhana was opened in August 2018, Governor of Texas Greg Abbott thanked the men and women in attendance for the 2,500 Ismaili volunteers who gave 13,000 hours of work toward recovery after Hurricane Harvey hit the Gulf Coast region of Texas.[7] Learning about this religious tradition was really inspiring, and it gave me a lot of respect for our friends who practice this faith.

Religious Diversity

Our children are growing up amidst not only growing racial and ethnic diversity, but also religious diversity. A single group of

---

[4]Ali Asani, "On Pluralism, Intolerance, and the Qur'an," *The Institute of Ismaili Studies,* https://iis.ac.uk/pluralism-intolerance-and-qur.

[5]Abdulaziz Sachedina, *The Islamic Roots of Democratic Pluralism* (New York: Oxford University Press, 2001), and Roy Mottahedeh, "Towards an Islamic Theology of Toleration," in *Islamic Law Reform and Human Rights*, ed. T. Lindholm and K. Vogt (Oslo: Nordic Human Rights Publications, 1992).

[6]There are approximately 1.5 billion Muslims in the world, most of them Sunnis, with only 10 percent being Shia. Ismaili Muslims are a little more than 10 percent of that Shia population according to John Harney, "How Do Sunni and Shia Islam Differ?" *The New York Times*, Jan. 3, 2016, https://www.nytimes.com/2016/01/04/world/middleeast/q-and-a-how-do-sunni-and-shia-islam-differ.html.

[7]Misbah Mukhi and Areebah Ajani, "Texas Governor and Community Officials Inaugurate New Ismaili Jamatkhana," *the.Ismaili*, August 22, 2018, https://the.ismaili/usa/texas-governor-and-community-officials-inaugurate-new-jamatkhana.

our children's friends may include a Muslim, a Jew, a Catholic, a Protestant, and someone whose family practices no religious faith.

The key word here is *practices*. In his book on identity, *The Lies That Bind,* Kwame Anthony Appiah shows how our ideas about what makes someone affiliated with a religion are often less about beliefs and more about practices. For an example, he cites the experience of Amartya Sen, an Indian economist and philosopher who grew up with a grandfather who was Hindu. As a teenager, Sen approached his grandfather and confessed that he did not believe in the Hindu gods. To this, his grandfather replied, "then you are an atheist Hindu." Even without believing in the doctrines of the religion, Sen could still be identified as a Hindu.[8]

Is Appiah right? Are religious identities more about practices than about beliefs? History seems to suggest otherwise. Religious wars have been waged over beliefs and differences in doctrine, and still today people choose to join one worshiping community rather than another over seemingly small differences. And yet to those persons who have left a church or synagogue over disagreements, these are not small issues.

Within my (Carolyn) own denomination, the Presbyterian Church (USA), there are a few things that make us distinct from other Presbyterians. For example, we ordain women and LGBTQ persons, two policies that are relatively recent (women have been ordained since the 1960s, and LGBTQ persons since the 2000s). These two differences alone have made for major controversies and arguments over the past several decades, with many church members and entire congregations leaving the denomination over these stances in the past decade.

As a member of this faith tradition, I am biased: I believe these issues to be central to my faith and have a hard time trusting persons who do not support women's ordination or the full inclusion of LGBTQ persons. I know enough history to be suspicious of religious claims that support excluding and stigmatizing whole groups of people, and I believe that the God who created this rich array of

---

[8]Kwame Anthony Appiah, *The Lies That Bind: Rethinking Identity* (New York: Liveright Publishing, 2018), 37.

diverse human beings intended for us to learn from our differences and not to hate one another for them.

And yet I have not always held these positions. My views have shifted over time, based on conversations with others and the opportunities I have had to know many LGBTQ persons of faith who felt called to ministry. There are many more people who are able to be out as gay or lesbian and serve in ordained ministry than there were when I was growing up, and there are many more resources available that point to religious affirmation of LGBTQ persons.[9]

Our religious traditions respond in different ways to social issues such as gender roles and sexual orientation, and religious groups are still trying to undo the damage from centuries of racism and its impact on segregation in religious communities. Christian churches are still learning from the mistakes they have made in perpetuating anti-Semitism and Islamophobia. While religious faith traditions can inspire us to be better people, they can also be the reason we use to justify mistreatment of one another. Some of the ways our religious traditions can harm one another can happen as early as children's religious education classes. If you are a Christian and grew up going to Sunday school, did your Sunday school teachers talk about "leaders of the Jews" persecuting Jesus? Or even more blatant anti-Semitism, describing Jews as being the ones who killed Jesus? Jewish author and New Testament scholar Amy-Jill Levine describes having had this experience growing up: another child accused her of killing God.[10] As a religious scholar who speaks to Christians about how to avoid anti-Semitism in the ways they teach the Bible, Levine points out that Jesus himself was a Jew, speaking with and to other Jews.

Returning to Appiah's idea about religious identity being about *practices,* I wonder if we can talk about religion with our children

---

[9]For example, see two books put out by my denomination's publishing house: Mark Achtemeier's *The Bible's YES to Same-Sex Marriage: An Evangelical's Change of Heart* (Louisville: Westminster John Knox Press, 2014) and Cody Sanders's *A Brief Guide to Ministry with LGBTQIA Youth* (Louisville: Westminster John Knox Press, 2017).

[10]Informal conversation between Levine and author, February 28, 2020.

and in our communities by way of naming the practices that are part of our traditions? For my family, I might name the weekly worship service we go to at church, and a Wednesday evening small group I attend with other adults while my kids are in youth programs. I might also point to the mission work our church is doing for the poor and homeless around Austin. I might point to the way we pray before meals; in these prayers we talk to God and give thanks for the things going well in our lives, and we lift up in concern the things that make us worry.

What are the practices that are part of the faith tradition in which you grew up? What did those practices look like? And are they things you are passing on to your children? Why or why not?

If you do not consider yourself religious, what are the practices in which you see your family engaging now that represent what you value? Do you bring your children with you to march in protests or to wait in long lines to vote, talking about why you value the democratic process?

Maybe it's the simple practice of having family meals together—a practice that is easier to say than it may be to schedule! Think about the ways you express your own values to your children, and let that be a jumping off point for talking about the diversity of faith traditions in your community.

The goal is not to know everything there is about different religions—we cannot possibly become experts in every faith tradition—but rather to be able to convey with respect the fact that some of our friends and neighbors practice a different faith than we do, and that such differences are nothing to fear but are instead opportunities for learning.

If you live in an area where there are other religious communities already doing interfaith work, perhaps you could introduce your child to people of different faiths coming together to have deeper relationships. One relationship in my city of Austin that has been in the news is between a black Baptist preacher, Daryl Horton, and a white rabbi, Neil Blumofe, who have taken two cross-country tours together to witness the history of African Americans and Jews living in America.[11] There are monthly events hosted by Interfaith Action of Central Texas to which persons can come to talk over dinner with people from different faith traditions about that month's topic.

Many children who grow up in certain religious traditions are confirmed or brought into the faith community as a full participant, typically as an adolescent. For Jews, these events are called bar mitzvahs (for boys) or bat mitzvahs (for girls). For many Protestants, there is confirmation. For Catholics, there is first communion. As persons of faith, these children are learning more about their specific tradition, practices, and beliefs. Some of their peers may be going through something similar in their own faith tradition. Helping youth understand religious diversity at this age as something that represents what their own family values, believes, and practices can equip them to see persons from other traditions as mysteries yet to be learned, future conversation partners, and as offering opportunities to become more familiar with one another within a diverse human family.

Joy Shares: Respecting the Differences, Honoring the Similarities

There are places where pluralism of different kinds has existed and continues to exist despite the challenges of difference.

My twenty-year college reunion just passed. I have particular memories of my time at Hobart & William Smith Colleges that I expect to keep for the rest of my life. One memory is the year I spent in Senegal, West Africa. There, I met a woman who has become one of my dearest friends. Pienda Diop Fall is Muslim. She prays several times a day, celebrates Ramadan, uses expressions such as "Inshalah." Yet I call her not just my friend but also my sister. Some people say we shouldn't be friends. Certainly, we have differing theological beliefs and even perspectives about life. Yet we have managed to maintain a friendship for more than twenty years. How?

---

[11]Daryl Horton and Neil Blumofe, "Commentary: Why We, a Reverend and a Rabbi, Travel to Witness America," Opinion, *Austin American-Statesman,* September 10, 2019, https://www.statesman.com/opinion/20190910/commentary -why-we-reverend-and-rabbi-travel-to-witness-america.

Why? We respect our differences and honor our similarities. We are simultaneously host and guest to each other.

Similarly, during my time in my doctoral program at Howard University I befriended a fellow resident assistant (R.A.), Camila Pereriera-Williams. She is Brazilian and of the Bahá'í faith. Camila and I have also maintained a friendship since graduating from Howard with our doctoral degrees even though she lives in Canada and I reside here in the United States. Camila and I also respect our differences and honor our similarities.

In the case of both these friends, our similarities are worth honoring while we respect our differences. What are our similarities?

We are all three women of color with a similar historical cultural context. We are all privileged to have received an education. We have all resided in the United States (although this happened at different times for all of us). And we each come from working- or middle-class families. Last, although we come from different faith traditions, all three of us share a strong spiritual compass, meaning that our faith decidedly affects our worldview and how we live.

I believe strongly that respecting difference and honoring similarities allows me to maintain relationships with people who are very different from me.

Balancing Respect for Our Differences and Honor for Our Similarities

Difference is not a new thing. No two persons are exactly alike—not even so-called identical twins! We are all unique in our own way. We must acknowledge our similarities along with our difference. It is by balancing these—respecting the differences and honoring the similarities—that we can form strong relationships across difference.

What does *respect* look like? What does *honor* look like?

RESPECT IS...

Respect does not mean agreement but *understanding,* which in part is a choice (i.e., I may not agree with what you believe but I can understand your line of thinking and why you believe as you do). Respect is allowing someone the choice not to participate or to participate with accommodations (think about special education, differently abled persons, multiple intelligences). Respect is empathetic.

Honor is...

Honor means affirming the humanity in persons regardless of identities (whether chosen by the individual or assigned/designated by society). Honor means highlighting aspects of one's humanity that is shared with another. Honor is choosing to connect with (an) other person(s).

While some people may focus on the many things that divide us as human beings, others prefer to honor the myriad attributes that make us similar. For example, we are born into families of one type or another. We begin as babies, dependent upon those who have come before us for nurture, education, and the like. As we become older, we learn what it means to be an adult and to be independent. We learn skills needed to survive in the context in which we reside. We experience the highs and lows of existing on planet Earth regardless of our ethnicity, religion, creed, or geographical location. We cry, we laugh, we wonder and dream. We desire more at some times and less at others. We crave for the opportunity and experience to belong, to be loved, and to love. Yet at some point our human bodies can take no more of this life—of the work that it requires to live—and we transition or pass on. Then those who are left grieve the physical presence of a loved one, while others maintain the belief that one is never really gone. Regardless of what you believe, death comes to us all. It does not respect race, class, or any social construction in which we place ourselves. We all bleed. We all die. This is the human cycle, the human story.

It is this common human cycle, this common human narrative that we must honor. The particularities of difference are important, and we need to respect those differences. However, we typically place too much emphasis on our differences and not enough on the things that unite us human beings as we attempt to thrive during our time here on planet Earth.

Perhaps if we honored our similarities a little more, we might argue less. There might be less war. People in positions of power might operate with a "do unto others" mentality and not take advantage of others. Perhaps if we honored our similarities more, we would share more—we would get to know our neighbors and those who are different from us.

Certainly, there is a need for balance. Focusing too much on either our similarities or our differences is problematic in that it ignores a particular aspect of who we are and what makes us who we are.

Respecting the differences means that we may be at different stations in life with different priorities. We may come from different cultures, eat different food, and listen to different music. Respecting the differences means that we may disagree on the best way to accomplish a goal or simply have different methods for achieving the same goal. There may be parts of our identity that matter more to us than they do to someone else.

Ultimately, by both respecting the differences and honoring the similarities, we can learn the balance together, and we can accommodate these growing pains with grace and strength.

Chapter 6 Activity for Self-Reflection

Personal Religiosity and Other Religions

Spend time thinking about the role of religion in your own life. Did you grow up in a house where one or both parents were people of faith? Did religious identity play a role in your own identity formation?

What were you taught early on about other religions? Did you have any friends who were from other faith traditions? Do you remember religion being something mentioned by other kids at school?

If you are not a religious person, what are your views of people who do practice faith? Are there certain beliefs that you hold that guide how you try to live your life and raise your children?

With regard to respecting the differences and honoring the similarities, what are the ways you are already doing this in your own life? As a parent or teacher, how do you see children respecting differences and honoring similarities? In the curriculum segment in the third Appendix, there are some suggestions of activities that can help children practice this themselves.

Returning to the *ABCs* of diversity, which religious identities make you feel *afraid? back up?* seek to *control* the situation by avoiding this person and their religion? Reflect on why these particular religious identities make you feel afraid. Are you afraid that their religious beliefs view your own identity in a negative way? If you are a woman encountering someone from a religious group that does not allow women in pastoral leadership, you may fear that this person does not see you as worthy. Take a moment to *acknowledge* the differences between you and try to focus on the practices of this person's religious faith. Are they still kind and respectful to you as a person? They may still *practice* respect toward you, even if their beliefs are different about the roles of women in the church. *Be present* to the discomfort you feel, and try to *come closer* in the relationship by honoring the similarities between you.

Write down your own experiences where the differences in religious identities have caused you to go into automatic ABCs, and how you might bridge to the intentional ABCs of interpersonal engagement. Take time to reflect upon the ABCs of a more just society as it relates to religious identities as well. Are there persecuted religious communities you are aware of? How can you *access* your own positions of privilege and show solidarity with friends in Jewish communities amidst anti-Semitic hate crimes? Can you *build* bridges to connect with Muslim communities in your area who feel threatened by Islamophobia? Seek to *cultivate* within yourself an appreciation for people of different faiths, learning from them how you can model interreligious respect and dialogue.

7

Social Media and Diversity

In June 2019, the Pew Research Center found that "seven-in-ten Americans use social media to connect with one another, engage with news content, share information and entertain themselves."[1] In twelve short years, the U.S. has gone from less than 20 percent of the population using the Internet and social media to about 70 percent of the population using the Internet and social media.[2] Yet many people are still unaware of the consequences of their technological usage and social media behavior *and* how it *impacts their lives off screen*. This Pew Research Center article also points out that it isn't just youth or young adults who are using the Internet and social media platforms. In fact, older adults (especially baby boomers) are increasingly using these platforms as well.

So? I hear you saying, dear reader. What does it mean that we spend so much time using media that reinforces the divisions between us?

Joy Shares: Technology and Social Media

I admit it: I love technology. Well, let me clarify. I, Joy, love the efficiency that technology can sometimes provide us. I recently upgraded to an iPhone 8 Plus. I know that may not sound to some like an upgrade, but I went from an LG2 that was three years old to an iPhone 8 Plus with all the bells and whistles. The people at T-Mobile informed me that the LG company was on the fifth iteration of its phone, which meant that my poor LG2, which I had

---

[1] Pew Research Center, "Social Media Fact Sheet," June 12, 2019, https://www.pewinternet.org/fact-sheet/social-media/.

[2] Pew Research Center, "Social Media Fact Sheet."

had for three years, was more than outdated. I was commended for having kept a phone that long!

One of the things I like about my new phone is the ability to take notes on it. There are times that I do not even use my laptop because I know I can open up OneNote and use it to write notes for students. This cuts down on my use of paper and enables me to have vital information right at my fingertips.

Confession: I was not great at email, and some might even say that I'm still not. I know how to *log off* and not just get off the computer but stay away from it. However, with my new phone I have this wonderful capability of having work stuff come right to it, and in that way, I've learned to be more attentive and responsive to my students when they have questions.

I also like technology in the kitchen. I'm currently eyeing one of those toaster/convection/air-fryers to make preparing dinner that much easier. I'm always looking for ways to be more efficient, and technology helps me do that.

But... (There's always a *but!*)

My little ones are currently five years old and three and a half years old, and they have had Kindles since they were toddlers. An aunt of mine sent them as a Christmas gift. Truthfully, I wasn't sure if it was a good idea or not. However, it became a saving grace; I went on YouTube and allowed Asa to watch nursery rhymes and rehearse his letters. At first I was surprised that Asa seemed to know how to turn on the Kindle and find his nursery rhymes without too much help from me—he was only about two years old. But then I remembered that my husband had treated himself to an iPad mini a few weeks before Asa was born. There are pictures of my husband holding both our infant son and his iPad. My kids were born with technology literally at their fingertips.

I noticed, too, that my daughter seemed to know that the videos on YouTube were a way for her to learn her colors, shapes, and numbers. I remember her sitting in her high chair in the kitchen while I was preparing dinner and hearing her repeat the words coming from the video on the screen—red, blue, and green.

I stopped what I was doing and walked over to her to see what she was looking at. Sure enough, she had managed to find videos and was studying her colors, shapes, and numbers without too much assistance from us. Now let me be clear: She goes to nursery school and is still rehearsing the foundations all children need to start kindergarten. However, as a parent I recognize that my children have *always* had technology at their fingertips. They do not know life without it. I have wondered about their screen time. Is it too much? Does it impair their learning? Research studies say both are true. Although I reasoned that if it was educational it might not be too bad, we did start to limit our children's access to technology because we found they would watch/interact with it for as long as we allowed them.

Today, I would say my children have a healthy relationship with technology. They use their Kindles, but they also value going to the library and taking out books, playing outside, participating in imaginary play, and playing with each other. Yes, they know the passcodes to get on the iPad, and most of the time they do not need any help from us. They watch *Ryan's Toy Review, JoJo Siwa, American Ninja Warrior Junior,* and other things I would have had *no clue* about had they not been watching it on YouTube. I still have to parent them, regardless of whether they are watching the Disney Channel or Nickelodeon on television or some YouTube star. Balance, in some form, is key. I see technology and social media as resources. They are not the only resources around, but they can be beneficial if used in the right way.

Now, with that said, let me take on the other side of the issue. In her book *Algorithms of Oppression,* Safiya Noble takes on the challenge of how algorithms used by social media platforms "reinforce oppressive social relationships and enact new modes of racial profiling."[3] Just as there has been *redlining* in the real estate and banking industries, Noble asserts that there has also been redlining in the digital world. For example, Noble's book emerged

---

[3]Safiya Noble, *Algorithms of Oppression* (New York: New York University Press, 2018), 1.

from her wanting to do something for her stepdaughter and some young family members, and when she searched for that topic on the web, it yielded porn. She couldn't believe it! Subsequent searches for other things yielded devastating results. It proved her theory. Humans are "developing the digital platforms we use;" thus, if they have bias (which they do), then what they produce also contains bias. How could we suppose anything different? How could something that is biased produce that which is not biased? Impossible. Exactly.

So while I like what technology enables me to do, I must also pause and ask how this reifies the challenges that I, as a black woman in America, already experience?

Joy Shares: The Privatization of Information

A couple of summers ago I attended the Institute for Research in African-American Studies at Columbia University for a summer teaching institute. Getting access to another institutional library made me giddy. Yes, I'm a nerd. However, as I endeavored to do my academic digging, I realized something: Information was, and is, becoming more privatized. I wondered why Columbia, like Princeton Theological Seminary and Princeton University—institutional libraries to which I currently have access—had so much more diverse collections than my local public library, or at least the central one. Even the most local branch, within walking distance of my New York apartment, is limited. When I wanted to conduct *research,* it seemed as if I had to have a connection to an institutional library in order to get anything done. Google Scholar, although helpful, was not going to cut it. In addition, I noticed that where I was physically located also affected my search results. Often I was between Princeton, New Jersey, and its adjacent town of West Windsor. Both of these spaces are affluent and teeming with dollars and affluence. When a person, group, or institution has affluence and resources, it affects the type of research they can do. For example, tuition at colleges and universities goes toward buying subscriptions to online digital subscriptions so that their patrons—college students, faculty, visiting scholars, and such— can have access to the articles produced. This is in addition to the physical collections that may be housed somewhere on a campus. However, public libraries rely on public funding—city, state, and maybe federal. In addition, they collect fees for late fines and other services. However, there is usually a huge difference between what you will find in terms of resources at an institutional library versus a public one. If you ever care to see what I am talking about, try going to an institutional library and then visit your local library. What differences do you notice? When I was in New Jersey doing research, I had access to institutional libraries, but my Internet searches came up different as well. My search results depended on my geography. Furthermore, when I found myself closer to where I spent most of my growing up, in Queens, New York, my search results varied considerably. I figure this has to do both with the relative lack of financial resources in Queens and with being in a community of color compared to Princeton. Which New York City borough I was in also affected my online research! It was then that I started acquiring multiple public library cards—first Queens (which was just a renew and reactivation), and then Brooklyn, and then New York Public Library. By gathering different library cards, I realized I could access a more diverse array of sources in hopes of producing better research. I knew that my children would also have access to different types of books because I have access via my library cards.

More recently, I decided to give my local central library another try. A lot had changed in the library since I had last hung out there in high school. It had *definitely* been upgraded. I'm not sure who was responsible for that, but from the bottom of my heart I thank you. I will be spending much, much more time in my local central library in the near future.

The takeaway from this anecdote is that information is definitely a commodity. This commodity is being influenced and impacted by the same structures that have marginalized individuals and whole communities that are different from those in positions of power.

While technology can assist us in making life better, we must also address the challenges it raises for us.

Bias, Bias Everywhere: Messages We Receive from Social Media

Imagine if everywhere you turned there was an obstacle. I mean everywhere: if getting a job, getting housing, buying food and clothes were all fraught with challenges because of the color of your skin or your religion or some other type of difference that makes you stand out. I know for a fact African Americans have lived through this struggle, and other marginalized groups have as well. Just being alive and attempting to live continues to be a challenge for many systemically oppressed groups in this country. The bias also extends to the Internet.

As adolescents go through puberty and experience their bodies changing, they continue to compare themselves to one another and evaluate themselves based on standards of beauty determined by their surrounding culture. With constant images of what counts as beautiful flooding their screens and devices, adolescents are inundated with people to whom to compare themselves. If a child does not match these images, it is easy for them to feel inadequate.

Parents can help youth by talking about the larger industries that benefit from our beauty insecurities—that advertising has always played to our self-perceptions by sending us the message "You too can look like this if only you buy our product!" In some ways, advertising has "tricked" us by telling us that our happiness and success in life are determined by how we look. By encouraging youth to see the "trickery" behind the constant images that try to sell us things, you can help them become more savvy in their own media consumption.

This kind of critical thinking is also important in regards to race. Invite your children to evaluate whether images they are seeing are perpetuating stereotypes of people groups, or whether producers of those images are representing only white people. One way of doing this is by asking, Are there only some kinds of identities represented in this show or movie? Another is by naming what we see: "I noticed the only person of color in this show is the Asian woman who runs a pizza restaurant, and she seems a bit crazy and angry. Do you think that the show writers are using a stereotype when they write her script? How would your friend who is Asian American feel about this character?" By giving youth the tools to evaluate media in this way, they begin to learn how to live in the world by embracing diversity and feeling as if something is amiss when it is not there.

Carolyn Shares: Social Media and Our Brain on "Likes"

The messages we receive about diversity that appear on television or in movies may feel a bit easier to critique than the subtle messages we receive through social media. Youth are able to send photos of themselves to their friends or out to the general public in hopes of getting "likes." The number of people who interact positively with a person's picture or post can affect how a young person feels about themselves. If no one comments on their post, they feel invisible. If only a few friends "like" the picture they posted of themselves, they wonder if they are attractive. They are also able to see pictures of their friends at parties or gatherings to which they may have not been invited, and "FOMO," or the "fear of missing out," becomes a constant obsession.

This isn't just a problem for youth, either. Adults also are susceptible, despite our best efforts. While working on this manuscript, I learned that an article for which I had been interviewed had been accepted by *Newsweek* magazine and was now on shelves.[4] This discovery happened on a day that I had intentionally reserved for all-day writing and research for this book. But how do you think my body felt after learning that my name and words would be in a national magazine to which I subscribed as a kid? Stress hormones immediately flooded my body. Stress can be both good and bad; happy things that happen to us can trigger stress, as can scary or bad things that happen to us. My brain was telling me, "Lots of

---

[4]Nadira Hira, "Why the Fight Against Racism Has to Start with Owning It," *Newsweek*, August 22, 2019. Available online https://www.newsweek.com/2019/08/30/fight-against-racism-owning-it-1455229.html.

people are going to be reading my name and what I said! What if they judge me? Or worse yet, want to harass me for my comments?" While it was exciting to be included, my brain also worried about what impact having my name in *Newsweek* would have on me emotionally and socially. So the brain set off an adrenaline flow.

With the adrenaline coursing through my system, my heart was beating faster and I wanted to do something. I wanted to reach out to the most important people in my life: my husband, my parents. I was out, writing away from home, and I was not able to reach my husband on the phone, which made me anxious. By this time, the cortisol was also kicking in, so I was feeling stressed by the experience. I also worried: "Will I get back to writing today?"

I wrote up a post on my website to share the article on social media, something from which I have generally stayed away during my writing process. Then I felt I had to put on my professional persona, so I changed my old profile pic from one with my daughter to the one I used on the back of my book. Then and only then I posted that I had been quoted in *Newsweek*!

Once I had shared the news with my friends and followers, another impulse set in: the "like" monitor. I found myself going back to social media sites to see who had "liked" the post; when the likes were not coming quickly, depression set in. "Should I have shared that article? Will my friends think I'm bragging? Is *Newsweek* really that big of a deal anymore?" So I went down a rabbit trail researching subscription numbers for *Newsweek* and read about its history of decline and tumult. I also noticed that at first I received more likes and comments about my profile picture than about the article in which I am quoted. "Hey!" I thought, "You're not supposed to like my appearance, but my ideas!"

This is our brain on "likes." We are interrupted from other trains of thoughts we may have been having, and instead our brain focuses on the virtual social interaction we are having with others who "like" us.

There is a reason for this. Whenever we get a "like" on social media, the brain sends out the chemical dopamine, which activates feelings of reward and pleasure.[5] Dopamine is the chemical in our brain that is deployed when we eat our favorite foods or have a successful day at work. It literally makes us feel good.

Unfortunately, this chemical can also be highjacked into patterns of addiction. Our brains want to be continually rewarded, but after a while those rewards may decrease. So social media platforms, which are paid for by advertisers, try to keep us coming back. Researcher Trevor Haynes wrote an article on dopamine and smartphones in which he mentioned the concept of "variable reward schedules," an idea originally discussed by behaviorist B. F. Skinner. Haynes says that we are more likely to keep coming back to look for rewards when we cannot predict when the rewards will be there.[6]

The article made me think about an app I use regularly, even though I would not otherwise be inclined to frequent this store: the Starbucks app. We have a local coffee shop that I prefer to support. So why do I instead regularly shop at Starbucks against my preference for local business? Because of their app. On some days, the app gives me the chance to earn 150 stars! All I have to do is buy something at the store three times in the next five days. It sounds easy enough, so I decide to do it. I could get the equivalent of a five-dollar beverage with that many reward stars, so I tell myself that it is worth it because I am "gaming the system."

Did you see what just happened? My brain gets tricked into thinking that I am getting away with something by earning a free five-dollar drink, when actually I am spending three times that amount over the next few days when otherwise I would not have gone out for coffee once. But my brain says, Spend fifteen dollars to get something worth five dollars for free? That sounds like a deal!

What makes it feel like more of a deal to my brain, and why I have to keep checking the app, is that this offer of 150 stars is not available every day. There are some days when no rewards are offered

---

[5]Trevor Haynes, "Dopamine, Smartphones & You: A Battle for Your Time," *Science in the News,* May 1, 2018, http://sitn.hms.harvard.edu/flash/2018/dopamine-smartphones-battle-time/.

[6]Haynes, "Dopamine."

other than the normal reward stars that accrue with any purchase. There are other days when a 30-star reward becomes available, and in my mind it seems not as worth it. So these variable rewards, coming in different amounts and on an unpredictable schedule, keep me coming back to an app and to a business that I would otherwise not frequent for coffee. This demonstrates the "variable reward schedule" concept Trevor Haynes was talking about.

Why is this important? Because we need to monitor our own dependence on "likes" and social media usage if we want our children to learn healthy habits from us.

University of Pennsylvania psychologist Melissa G. Hunt conducted a study of students' experiences with depression and loneliness.[7] Her findings point to increased feelings of depression and loneliness when students spend more time on social media platforms. When students were required to limit their use to only ten minutes a day, they were noticeably less depressed and less likely to say they felt lonely.

This makes sense. Social media enables us to present our best selves to the world: our most attractive photos, our most exciting vacations, the tastiest meals and fanciest restaurants and shows we enjoy. When we are looking at the highlight pictures and vacations and experiences of so many others, our view of reality can become distorted. We begin thinking that everyone looks that good (except for me). We assume everyone is taking such luxurious vacations (except for us). We see all the fun others are having and we feel left out (what's wrong with me?). The comparisons we make between ourselves and others can lead to feelings of loneliness, inadequacy, and a general dissatisfaction with our own lives: "Why can't my life be like this other person's?"

Even though limiting social media use is associated with increased feelings of well-being, we still find it hard to stick to such limits ourselves. Returning to the dopamine loop in our brain,

---

[7]Michele W. Berger, "Social Media Use Increases Depression and Loneliness," *Penn Today,* November 9, 2018, https://penntoday.upenn.edu/news/social-media-use-increases-depression-and-loneliness, citing Melissa G. Hunt, et al. "No More FOMD: Limiting Social Media Decreases Loneliness and Depression." *Journal of Social and Clinical Psychology,* vol. 37, No. 10, 2018, 751-68.

we are hard-wired to look for rewards; and when we are not sure where to find them, we go to places where we have found them before. If we are feeling bored or lonely, we may be motivated to get on social media because by doing so we have the experience of feeling connected to friends who live far away, and that has felt good in the past. But we cannot count on our social media experience feeling good all of the time. If you have exciting news to share with others (like I did), you may feel the impulse to tell your friends on social media because of a past positive experience of feeling that other people were celebrating your successes with you. But again, you cannot count on every experience being positive, such as when I felt offended by friends more frequently liking my updated profile picture than the link I had shared about being quoted in *Newsweek*.

To be fair to my friends, within an hour of posting the likes for my link to *Newsweek* soon outnumbered the likes of my profile photo. But to say that I noticed this, and that I counted the likes (22 and 20, respectively), shows just how hooked into this dopamine reward loop I am, even as I write about the importance of limiting our social media time! So I am the first to acknowledge that moderation is easier to talk about than to practice.

Carolyn Shares: Social Media and Politics

Besides doing powerful things to our brain, social media also does powerful things to our society and our politics. Social media sites enable people to share articles from across the Internet, from reputable news sites to videos people uploaded at home onto YouTube. What is shared is often a representation of one's own political position, and where we get our media often depends upon whether we are a Republican or a Democrat. And because it is so easy to create content online and make it seem real to others, people have used the Internet to spread stories about people and political policies that are not accurate.

I (Carolyn) come from a big family, and I have many nieces and nephews. At a family reunion, I had an opportunity to sit with a table full of them and asked them a question: "How can you use your creative talents to solve the world's problems and work for social justice?"

Silence filled the table as they considered my ridiculously difficult question. My nieces and nephews ranged in age from nine to nineteen, with all of them generally fitting within the stage of adolescence. They looked similar in some ways, their physical characteristics a beautiful mix of my sisters and brothers-in-law, and they all lived in different parts of the state of Texas. Some lived in San Antonio and had other relatives in the suburbs of Houston and Fort Worth, while others lived in smaller Texas towns. And yet despite the similarities of having come from the same family and living in the same state, they had very different perspectives in response to my question.

One responded, "You know, I'm not sure I can answer that. It's a lot of pressure. I feel like older generations have done a lot to mess up this world, and now they're looking to us and saying, 'You fix it.' I don't think that's fair. I don't think that's our job."

Another said, "I'm thinking about joining the military after high school."

Still another asked me, "Well, what do you mean, exactly? Because there's a lot of things that people consider to be a problem, that other people don't. Like some people consider being gay or lesbian is a problem, or not including them is a problem, and then there are other people who kind of make a big deal about animals, and they want everyone to call them by their furry name."

"*Furry* name? What's that?" I asked, never having come across that term before.

"You don't know what a furry is? Oh, it's all over the Internet. It's like people who love animals and think they're an animal, and they want you to call them by their animal name. There's a kid at my school who's a furry, and they always wear cat ears and think they're a cat. So I mean, like, if everybody has to have their own identity and gets to choose what they want to be, then where do you stop? Do we have to call everybody by whatever thing they want to be seen as?"

I had known these kids since they were babies. I know my sisters well, and I thought I knew something about adolescents. But this conversation baffled me. We soon got into a more political discussion, and the kids had political opinions about issues ranging from gun control to abortion, and they wanted me to view videos they could pull up on their phones that had solidified in their mind the rightness of their own position. I was out of my league.

I was baffled because these youth had very different opinions on issues that I cared about, and several of them already had firmly formed opinions about political issues that I thought only adults talked about. As someone who lives in a city known for being liberal, I could see how living in different parts of the same state meant we were imbibing very different politics.

It also taught me that kids are picking up a lot from the Internet. They get their information from online sources and take seriously the opinions and views that confirm their own perspectives. Scholars have called this "confirmation bias," in that we are more likely to agree with perspectives that confirm what we already believe. Liberals and conservatives both have this bias; liberals get their media from sources that conservatives consider liberal, and conservatives get their news from sources that liberals consider conservative.

As with younger children, adolescents are never "blank slates" just waiting for adults to inform them how to view the world around them. They are constantly making up their own minds, choosing to engage in some forms of media rather than others, engaging with the perspectives of their friends online, and selectively taking in messages from their families and communities as they relate to what they learn from the Internet.

This experience also activated for me the automatic ABCs of diversity discussed earlier in the book, beginning with the unhelpful forms: being Afraid, Backing away, and Control. I felt afraid, not in some terrorized sense, but in an "I'm in over my head" kind of way, and I was afraid of feeling uncomfortable. I realized I had different opinions on issues important to me, and that made me afraid to share my perspectives with these nieces and nephews. So in a sense, I "backed away"; I became quiet as I listened to them, not knowing what to say. I also made a move toward "control" by eventually inserting myself back into the conversation to direct the topic. I wanted to control what we were talking about so it would no longer make me feel discomfort about our different perspectives.

What would it have looked like for me to have experienced the more positive reactions to difference? I could have brought to mind the intentional engagement or personal ABCs of Acknowledging, Being present/curious/willing to make mistakes, and Coming closer to the conversation. I needed to *acknowledge* that my nieces and nephews had different opinions, and that this challenged me. I needed to *be present* to my feelings of insecurity and uncertainty, and I could have *come closer* to them by asking follow-up questions to try to learn more about their point of view, rather than trying to shift the conversation away to something easier to discuss.

One of the realities of our growing polarization as a country is that we are going to have different political opinions than other people. This is shaped by our sources of media and by the information on which we rely to tell us about the world. It is also shaped by our community—what are the norms and ideas held by our parents and other important figures in our lives? And it is shaped by our own individual interests and concerns.

In our polarized society, our politics often determine how we interpret issues of diversity. There are persons on the right who argue that valuing all diversity must mean valuing the right to speak freely against certain groups, and that requiring businesses to serve gay couples, for instance, infringes on their right to freely practice their religion, which they see as condemning homosexuality. There are persons on the left who argue that including and valuing diversity needs to have a central place in our society, but that the forms of speech that they consider to be hate speech should not be seen as another form of diversity, but rather as an attempt to discriminate against persons marginalized by society.

We may not have all of the answers about how to live as one community in what Martin Luther King Jr., called this "world house," but having conversations with people face to face, as opposed to only over social media, is essential. We need to be able to get beyond the screens that give us information that only tells part of the story. We need to sit at table with people who have different opinions on things, and we need to practice the language of diversity.

Chapter 7 Activity for Self-Reflection

Our Online Presence and Community

Where do you spend your time online? What are your sources for news? Which online site do you frequent to find out what is going on in the lives of your friends and family?

How does your activity online mirror your own community? Are the people with whom you talk or interact online the same people with whom you tend to spend time in person?

How does the feedback loop of "likes" affect your activity online? Do you notice any changes to how you feel after being online? If so, when, and why?

What are the messages you receive implicitly about yourself and people who look and think like you from being online? What do you learn about people who are different from you by being online?

After responding to these questions, put your answers into conversation with the interpersonal ABCs of diversity. What do you learn about *access* from being online? What opportunities do you have to *build* connections and relationships through social media? In what ways can you *cultivate* interactions with people who are different from you through social media that could lead to in-person relationships that build trust and mutual learning?

Old Enough to Know Better

Many people would be scared if they saw in the mirror not their faces—but their character. —Unknown

The above statement is arresting, isn't it? Sit with it for a moment. What kind of character do *you* see when you look in the mirror? Let me suggest that when most of us look in the mirror, we see hard working people, *decent* people. We see the reflection of persons who go to work, or work from home, and provide for their families. We see the reflection of persons who participate in community and civic events. We see the reflection of persons who donate their time to the local soup kitchen or an afterschool program. Yet this statement goes further, deeper. This statement addresses not what shows up on the surface, although it can be indicative of what is underneath, but rather the source of our behavior—our thoughts, conscious and subconscious, and our intentions.

Nowadays, we have the ability to alter our image—both the physical one and the one projected on social media. We can be—or at least project—almost anything we want. Yet this statement gets at the character issues—the things that cannot be seen, the intentions and motives—and it says that many people would be afraid. Given the current events in our country and our world, perhaps this statement is not so far off. However, there is still hope. There is still possibility!

Youth are learning each and every day from parents, grandparents, aunts, uncles, teachers, religious leaders, and neighbors about the world in which they live and their place in it. They learn from us. Perhaps if we change, if we adjust, if we pivot, then maybe, just maybe, they will do the same. The next generation cannot become the next generation without us. This is without a doubt a partnership, not a competition.

Actions Speak Louder Than Words: Understanding Ethics and Morals

It's true: Actions do speak louder than words. How one behaves is much more an indicator of what one believes than what one says. From a communication perspective, a groundbreaking study by anthropologist Ray Birdwhistell says that most of our communication—two thirds of it actually—is non-verbal.[1] The remaining one third is verbal. So what we say confirms what we have already demonstrated in our actions. Everything we say and do communicates something. Our words reinforce our actions—public and private.

Do you have a faith tradition? (Don't worry, I'm not attempting to proselytize.) For those of us who claim a faith tradition, there are tenets of these faiths that should guide us in our treatment of others, especially those who are different from us. Nevertheless, even if you do not adhere to any particular faith tradition, I'm sure there are some principles or guidelines that you follow for living your life. This is what it means to have morals (and ethics).

Ethics refers to "the theory of proper human conduct."[2] A more simplistic definition is that it involves attitudes and actions that are considered to be right or wrong. Morals or moral—in Latin, *moralis*—refers to manners. When I was growing up, my mother would call it *common courtesy*. From a communications standpoint or even a human standpoint, it is acknowledging the humanity of the person with whom you enter into a communicative exchange—whether that it is acknowledging their presence via a greeting or holding the door as a person passes through. Moral philosophy

---

[1]Ray Birdwhistell, *Introduction to Kinesics: An Annotation System for Analysis of Body Motion and Gesture* (Louisville: University of Louisville, 1979).

[2]Kelly James Clark et al., *101 Key Terms in Philosophy and Their Importance for Theology* (Louisville: Westminster John Knox Press, 2004).

more specifically refers to the examination of human behavior in terms of what is right or wrong.

Ethics and morals are terms that you may have heard in your civics class. Or perhaps in a philosophy class in college. Often the terms *ethics* and *morals* are used interchangeably. However, ethics is a set of moral principles. It is a code of conduct, whereas morals or morality has to do with the rightness or the wrongness of one's actions. Ethics answers questions about what principles or guidelines one follows in the world. Morals answers questions relating to how right or wrong those guidelines or principles tend to be.

We all grow up with some moral and ethical principles by which we guide our lives. These may be expressed in a religious tradition or through spiritual practices. Whether you are part of an institutional religious group or you simply believe in *doing the right thing,* then you have (in theory) an ethic. Now, it is one thing to have a belief or code of ethics by which you say you live. It is another to live out the morals or ethics you say you have. To be sure, there are situations that will challenge those morals and ethics. But as a whole, do you try to live out your morals and ethics?

In the field of psychology there is a theory called "cognitive dissonance theory," first proposed by psychologist Leon Festinger. The theory holds that when people experience psychological conflict, they attempt to reduce the conflict in order to restore balance or harmony to their emotional state. Many people like to think of themselves as consistent and true in all things, yet the reality is that when there is a conflict between belief or action, the automatic response is to find a way to justify either the belief or the action in some way.

This is a hard truth that few of us can handle. I'm hoping that you can and will. It says that many people believe that they are one way, but if they took some time to analyze themselves, if they took some time to give themselves a good once-over in the mirror, there's a good chance that they would not like what they see. There are many people who learn to see the good in people, and I think that can be useful and valuable. However, who we are is demonstrated not just in the things we think or even say but principally in the things we actually do, in the policies we support, in who our friends are or are not. Those actions are the things we really mean. From a communications perspective we communicate to the world all the time that we are afraid to look into this mirror of truth. Sure, we all have our faults. We don't always put things back where they belong. Or we leave the cart out at Target instead of walking it back to the store. These are things that don't make us bad people. But the moment our car gets struck by the stray cart, or we go to look for something and can't find it because someone didn't put it away properly, aren't we up in arms? There is a lack of consistency in what we say we believe and our behavior. This difference between our beliefs and our behavior is what we call "cognitive dissonance."

Microaggressions and Shifting

Our behavior can hurt people and have real consequences in the lives of others. It isn't just the things we *say* but the things we *do*. Now, it doesn't mean that people have not learned to survive. But consider how you would feel if you were a member of a group that was consistently disliked and daily threatened with violence. Some people live with this fear every day.

The book *Shifting: The Double Lives of Black Women in America* by Charisse Jones and Kumea Shorter-Gooden is a study conducted by two black women of almost 500 black women across the United States. Jones and Shorter-Gooden examined how race played into the lives of these women and what impact it had. They developed a theory they called "shifting."[3] And their study proves this theory. Shifting is a strategy that describes both internal or external moves that black women make to deal with the challenging images and expectations of society. Women *shift* in order to survive. Shifting is literal and metaphorical. Shifting is done both inwardly and outwardly. It is the lowering of the eyes. It is the sinking feeling that comes from being infringed upon yet again and making the decision to speak up—even if it costs. It is the way a woman vacillates between being angry and wondering if she should be angry at all.

---

[3]Charisse Jones and Kumea Shorter-Gooden, *Shifting: The Double Lives of Black Women in America*, (New York: HarperCollins, 2003).

Shifting is how black women and other marginalized groups deal with microaggressions.

What is a "microaggression"? The term's originator was a Harvard professor and psychiatrist named Chester M. Pierce back in 1970. Psychologist Derald Wing Sue picks up the term and adds some specificity to it for our time,[4] noting that "microaggressions are the everyday slights, indignities, put-downs, and invalidations that people of color experience in their day-to-day interactions with well-intentioned and well-meaning people who are unaware that they have delivered a put-down or invalidation."[5]

In an interview on *PBS News Hour,* Derald Wing Sue explained how these microaggressions are part of the everyday experiences of people of color. The interview took place when explicitly racist comments were being directed at students of color at the University of Missouri. The interviewer raised critiques, saying people objected to the word "microaggression" because it seemed to coddle children who just needed to get a tougher skin for the real world. To these criticisms, Sue responded: "The problem is that people believe microaggressions are very similar to the everyday incivility and rudeness that individuals, white Americans, experience in their day-to-day lives. They are quite different. Microaggressions for people of color are constant, continual, and cumulative. They occur to people of color from the moment of birth to when they die. And, as a result, any one microaggression in isolation may represent the feather that breaks the camel's back. And people who don't see the lived experience of people of color and the daily onslaught that they experience tend not to believe that it's a major event."[6]

The reason why they are all such big events is that a single microaggression communicates a much bigger message. Sue

[4]Derald Wing Sue, *Microaggressions in Everyday Life: Race, Gender and Sexual Orientation* (Hoboken, N.J.: John Wiley & Sons, 2010).

[5]Derald Wing Sue, "Microaggressions in His Own Words," interview posted online by the Collaborate Agency Group. Available online: https://www.youtube.com/watch?v=-_ltWFYVW2Y .

[6]*PBS NewsHour* interview November 13, 2015 with Derald Wing Sue, available online at https://www.pbs.org/newshour/show/how-unintentional-but-insidious-bias-can-be-the-most-harmful.

suggests that the person who asks him, "Where are you from?" is trying to make a personal connection. But when he answers, "Portland, Oregon," and they insist on asking where he is "really" from, the message they are sending is that he is not a true American, and that he will always be seen as a foreigner in the country he was born in.[7]

Microaggressions are often blamed on the perception of the individual, and persons may go so far as to insist that the comment "go back to your country" is not racist.[8] To be sure, some microaggressions are not direct, but even if indirect, they are often leveled on purpose. This is how racism has continued to maintain its presence in a morphed form.

Racism has been able to hide in political correctness and now in microaggressions. Because microaggressions seem so "small" or insignificant to outsiders, and the people who commit microaggressions are often "well-meaning," it can seem that these acts are justified or innocent, and that the victims are crazy and the aggressions are not real, just in their heads. Whether or not a person admits to committing microaggressions against another person, the reality is that they can be felt. For example, the grabbing of the purse, the inching in front of a person, the aggressive driving, the smart comments, the retorts—all of the ways that persons are made to feel less than, or perhaps at fault for simply *being*—all these are microaggressions. When someone is wronged, being made to feel as if it is no big deal is an act of microaggression. So is always having to adjust and deal with commentary that is disrespectful, rude, or hurtful.

How can we say we live by a code of ethics or a sense of morals when our actions suggest otherwise? How can it be that we do the opposite of what we say we believe? We all experience dissonance at some point on some level. However, it is imperative that we go beyond just what is comfortable for us.

---

[7] *PBS NewsHour* interview November 13, 2015.

[8] Katie Rogers and Nicholas Fandos, "Trump Tells Congresswomen to 'Go Back' to the Countries They Came From," *New York Times,* July 14, 2019, https://www.nytimes.com/2019/07/14/us/politics/trump-twitter-squad-congress.html.

Joy Shares: Invisible at the Party

I have dealt with and continue to deal with microaggressions related to race. This summer my kids left Queens and went to a camp out on Long Island, New York. By all accounts my children had a great first-time camp experience, and I plan to send them back when the finances allow. I sent my kids there because the camp seemed to offer a true camp experience that I desired for my children to have. They were safe. They interacted with persons different from them and had experiences that I would like to give them myself. This was a great way for them to experience some new things. I was able to check out the camp online and then by visiting it. I had a good idea as to what kind of environment I was sending my children into, and I thought it would be a good two-week experience.

For clarity, I identify as an African American woman, and my husband is a Caribbean man—or Jamaican to be exact. So while most people would see us as black or from the African diaspora, which we proudly are, we also come from two different ethnic backgrounds. It is an intercultural marriage.

My kids are African American and Caribbean, and they were the only children of color in their groups at camp—at least from what I could tell. At least visibly, they were the only black children.

One of my son's camp mates had a birthday party. We went. Although my husband and I didn't talk a whole lot about it, we had a pretty good idea of what we would experience, and we weren't that far off. With the exception of approximately four or at most six people, no one talked to us at all. And honestly, I was and am over attempting always to be the bridge. It is exhausting. The women, and in particular the white women, were the worst.

To their credit, the parents of the birthday boy made a sincere effort at schmoozing with everyone. However, I got the sense that the mother, and the father too, knew the challenges that we would experience. It was a two-hour child's party at a seemingly fun facility. The two hours were *more* than enough. The kids seemed to have a good time, but socially, it was definitely too much for the adults.

Interestingly, the sister of the father, who was of Hispanic descent, came and talked with me. She explained that she had told her sister-in-law that she would no longer go to the kid parties with her due to the social challenges that she experienced at them, socioeconomically and culturally. We chatted, had good conversation, and even hugged goodbye. In stark contrast, I believe only two white men spoke to my husband and me. With the exception of the sister of the father, the babysitter, and those two men, everyone else acted as if we didn't exist. And again, our children were visibly different from everyone else there.

I think there is something to be said for being visibly different—whether that is due to skin color or some other feature that can be seen. Some features draw attention—or are more socially acceptable—while others are not. Sometimes features that would naturally repel get bumped up the social ladder if there are other more intolerable visible differences. With that said, there are people who get to pass because their differences do not show up or are not easily detectable.

Let me explain. Perhaps no one ever actually says that they do not like you. However, when you walk into a room and it is not welcoming, you feel it. You can feel hostility, you can feel dislike. And the microaggressions that come with that are *real*.

For example, there is no common courtesy. People stand directly in passageways—almost on purpose—and when they see you approaching, they don't move. However, I am sure that most of the people, the women in particular, would think of themselves as good people. Yet in that space they did not consider me to be a mother. They did not perceive my husband and me as a happy couple accompanying our children to another child's birthday party. We were black...and that was it. Just black...nothing else, nothing more.

Even though we are of African descent, *we are also and foremost human beings*. In addition to being of African descent, we are also husband and wife, mother and father, college-educated, hard working. What I am saying? Yes, I am black. We are proudly black.

But you can't stop there. We are black and a list of other things—just like you. We must acknowledge difference, but we can't stop there. When we do, we actually hurt both parties—not just the person or persons to whom the microaggressions are directed. There are people and spaces that are waking up to this fact that everyone loses out when we judge, execute, and sentence people by their skin color alone, or for any difference that does not line up with what we have been taught or who we think we are.

Talking Across Our Differences: Being a Good Host and Guest

In order to have a hospitable situation, you have to have a willing hostess and a willing guest. If there is neither a willing host nor a willing guest, then you cannot have a nice visit. Both are integral to the success of good company. The same is true when talking across differences...you have to have willing parties to navigate. One person is not enough.

In order to engage in talking across differences, there need to be some guidelines. The idea of being a good host and guest is something familiar the world over, so perhaps we can start with that.

In order to talk across difference successfully, there needs to be a good host and a good guest.

A good host is someone who desires to make another person welcome and comfortable with the means that they have. This entails forethought, planning, and preparation. Once the guest arrives, the host is attentive to the needs of the guest, even at the risk of neglecting her own needs. Usually, this means providing the guest space to put down their luggage, clean up, and rest. Then there is the offering of some type of refreshment or meal because, let's face it, it's easy to work up an appetite while traveling.

Once the guest has had an opportunity to collect herself, then the real visit can begin! The venturing out and seeing of sights, the late-night conversations over tea or coffee, or sitting on the couch and looking through old photos. There is a process even when we visit with friends and family. We are delighted to see them, but in order to enjoy them, and in order for them to enjoy us, there is process. This process is the meeting of their needs as human beings. This is necessary for people who may be similar to us as well as for those who are different from us.

However, being a good host also requires a *good guest*. I say a good guest, because a good guest recognizes when a hostess is doing her best—and is willing to work with that. A good guest recognizes what the hostess can do, and perhaps what the hostess cannot do.

For example, on a trip to India, when I (Joy) reached my final destination, I hopped off the van to check out my living quarters in the retreat center. I found my room—it had my name on it—and headed for the bathroom. It looked like a bathroom, except the shower was not quite a shower. I was in the mountains and, well, it was a dip-the-dipper-into-the-bucket-and-throw set-up. I had hot and cold water, most of the time, which I collected in a bucket. Then, after soaping up, I washed myself off by throwing water over myself using the dipper.

I've lived abroad before, but I am American, and it had been a long time since I had done this sort of thing, so I needed to adjust mentally again. My shock lasted a few moments, and then I remembered where I was: in the mountains of India at a retreat center. I recognized that being a good guest would mean I would be soaping up, dipping, and throwing for the next couple of weeks because this was the best that our hosts could do for us.

Complaining about a situation like this would not have been helpful for me or my hosts. It would have made me look like the Ugly American, and it would have been offensive to my hosts because they were offering me what they had.

Again, being a good guest means recognizing what your host can and perhaps cannot do.

This extends to conversations as well. In the world of education, we like to talk about schema. Schema refers to prior knowledge or experience. It is the foundation necessary to be able to understand a particular concept. This book has endeavored to provide a schema for helping us talk about the differences that exist among us.

Conclusion: Choosing Our Place in History

What side of history do you want to be on?
—Angela Rye, political strategist and advocate

Political commentator Angela Rye often asks fellow political commentators, "What side of history do you want to be on?" Indeed, it is a critical question, one that the respondent may not be able to answer at the moment. And I don't think Angela expects them to answer that question right then and there. The question is a growing-pain moment. It is injected into the conversational atmosphere and hangs there.

I believe Angela seriously wants them to think about it. Meditate on it. Search their insides and reflect on what they say they believe and the policies they advocate. This doesn't mean that critical self-reflection will lead you to a different place. But critical self-reflection should lead you to a *deeper* place—and hopefully a more *informed* place—on important issues. This question has continued to resonate in me regularly. And so now, I pose it to you, dear reader.

Dear mother, father, sister, brother, uncle, auntie, pastor, rabbi, imam, or teacher, I ask you, "What side of history do you want to be on?"

You don't need to have a well-thought-out answer right now. But it should be a question that you begin thinking about and perhaps revisit from time to time. It is a question we should all think about to help us make better decisions about how we are going to navigate this watershed moment in history—not simply on a societal level but also on a daily personal level.

In fact, you have already made a decision about what side of history you desire to be on by reading this book.

Your decision to inform yourself, learn more, and figure out how to engage difference is important. Do not take it lightly. Some people would rather stick their heads in the sand and hope that this moment in time blows over. It won't. As a matter of fact, it will never ever be the same again.

This is crucial. There are critical moments in history, and we are definitely in one such moment. It is imperative to think about where you stand in it—where you *want* to stand in it. Once the moment passes, what you could have or should have done won't matter. In fact, it will be irrelevant. *All that matters is what actions you engage in to be better in the present and move forward.*

Our children and their children will inherit what we do—or do not do. So, in the words of Angela Rye, I ask again, "What side of history do you want to be on?"

I know I would like to be on the side of history that says something, that makes a difference—not just in word but also in deed—and that gives my children, and others, the tools they need to navigate this already-here, right-now society.

The reason why we want to talk about this concept of "diversity" is because there is a history in this country of violence against persons who are in the minority or who are seen as "other" or "inferior," or just "different."

What talking about our differences does is to make those "others" less scary to persons who may fear what is different, in the hopes that if those persons have the power to harm others, they will make a different choice, a choice for the other's good and for their well-being. And maybe talking about our differences and our history of violence as a country can inspire us to stand up for people who are seen as different, and our children will continue to engage and embrace difference.

We are a country of resilience and of change. African Americans have managed to thrive in a country that forcibly removed them from their ancestral heritage and enslaved them for hundreds of years.

Persons who are seen as "perpetual foreigners," persons of Asian descent or people of color from around the world who bring with them their accents and unique heritage, have managed to make this country their own and contribute to its success.

Persons who are gay or lesbian or transgender or non-binary are making progress in receiving the recognition they deserve as Americans who also make up the beauty of the diversity that is the United States.

And white people are learning about racism and supporting the work of persons of color who are leading the way in fighting for the rights of all marginalized communities.

Religious leaders of all faiths are reaching out to one another, seeing the importance of interfaith dialogue and cooperation. When a church, synagogue, or mosque is vandalized or targeted for a hate crime, the other communities of faith in the area express their solidarity and ask, "How can we stand with you?" We are learning how to support one another amidst our diversity in this wide, wonderful world of ours.

And even across our political divide, as deep as it seems to be, there are individuals building bridges, emphasizing common goals rather than partisan interests. Of course, more can be done here, and in every other area of embracing our diversity and working together. To say we are making strides is not to say we have arrived, but that we have reason to hope.

All of us can be part of this movement to make America the land of the free and home of the brave. It is going to take bravery. And it is a return to the original intentions of the men who wrote our Constitution, believing that all people are born with inalienable rights: to life, liberty, and the pursuit of happiness. But we can't get there by hiding in cabinets or looking through windows at what others are doing. We have to be out there in the world, learning skills to work together to build community and ensure the mutual success of all of our citizens. That is the dream. And it starts with us waking up, choosing what side of history we want to be on, and getting to work.

Acknowledgments

I (Carolyn) would like to begin by thanking Joy for her willingness to jump into this project with me. A little backstory: Joy and I met for the first time more than a decade ago on the campus of Princeton Theological Seminary. She and I were classmates, but we did not keep in touch. Fast-forward to 2018, when we crossed paths again a little over a year ago at our academy guild meeting, the Academy of Homiletics. This is the conference where faculty members who teach preaching or speech at theological schools or seminaries gather to talk about current and ongoing research. Joy and I literally ran into each other on the way to the women's restroom. We got to talking in the hallway about where our lives had taken us since we had last seen each other: I had gone on to study racism and teach preaching at Austin Seminary, and she had gone on to study intercultural communication and teach speech at Princeton Seminary. We talked about being moms and the challenges of the academic life while raising children. She shared with me she had previous teaching experience in public schools before going into academia and having kids, so in some ways she was prepared. And then it came out:

"Do you want to write a book together?"

I had been speaking to groups of people about racism since my first two books came out in 2018: *Anxious to Talk about It: Helping White Christians Talk Faithfully about Racism*, and a book for preachers: *Preaching about Racism: A Guide for Faith Leaders*. The first book tried to acknowledge the challenges of talking about racism by naming some of the feelings, such as anxiety, that often come up for people (particularly white people) when talking about racism. The second book was more technical, looking at biblical interpretation and theological perspectives that preachers could draw from to talk about racism with their congregations.

As I spoke about these books in churches and at conferences parents asked me: "How do we talk about these things with our kids?" I was also becoming aware of the challenge of talking about other forms of diversity with my kids, such as gender and sexuality, and I was not sure how these things were being talked about in school. So I wanted to learn from another teacher. Because Joy had a background as a public school teacher, I felt confident her experience would contribute many of the missing pieces my background lacked.

But Joy and I had never before worked together, had never taught together, and were not even that close as individuals. How would we make this work? We started by getting together over videoconferencing, meeting once a week to talk, brainstorm, and share some of our thoughts and ideas about the project. We were able to meet up in Princeton at the beginning of the summer when I flew up to lead a workshop there. During our time together we crafted a draft for our table of contents and divided up the work.

What really gelled our writing was when Joy hosted me at her home in Queens in September. I had the privilege of getting to meet her sweet children, who generously showed me their toys and favorite books, as well as her kind husband. Joy took me around the neighborhood, and the weather was perfect. I got to see her garden plot in the community garden and meet some of her neighbors. It was a real treat.

I also realized while we were together that this book we were writing was something Joy was already living. She was interacting with people from different cultures every day, and as a black woman, she was embodying "diversity" for others. I am really grateful for her willingness to share her experiences in these pages, for my benefit, and for the benefit of others like me. And for my part, as a white person, I know it is also the job of white people to "do our own work," and to do the work of talking about diversity with others, so the task is not always delegated to people of color. But I know I do this work imperfectly, and my whiteness limits what I can see sometimes, and so it is really helpful to get to share this writing experience with Joy.

There are other people I'd like to thank, including Brad Lyons and Deb Arca at Chalice Press, as well as Gail Stobaugh, Hui-Chu Wang, and our editor, Ulrike Guthrie. Thanks for the work all of you have put into bringing this to life! I also want to thank all of the moms and dads who are working to talk to their kids about our differences in positive ways: in particular, Rachel and Han Tjoeng, Melva Sampson and Derrick Young, Kim Taylor and Spencer Miller-Payne, Jen and Brian Hunt, Margaret Aymer and Laurent Oget, and so many others who have inspired me by their parenting and teaching. I want to thank my own children for their great feedback (they wanted me to include a section on "When parents say things that embarrass their children," but that will have to wait for the website). And finally, Phil: thank you for your tireless support, your taking on added responsibilities so I could "bust this out" again and again every time a new deadline appeared, and for your amazing skills as a parent in helping our children appreciate the differences all around us. And to you, dear reader, thank you. Thanks for working to make this world a better place by reading this book and making a difference where you can. Every bit helps, so thank you, and keep up the good work.

I (Joy) would like to thank Carolyn for this project. Talk of bringing unity where others seek to maintain the status quo and keep the divide can be risky business, but you desire to do that and more. It is a pleasure to know you and call you friend. I would also like to thank Carolyn for being an ally and attempting to live what she teaches and preaches in public for the world to see. You are an example for those who desire to be true conduits of justice and grace—not just in theory but in thought, word, and deed. Thank you for listening, leaning in, and even getting on a plane to come to

New York so that we could work together in person! I am in awe of your energy and dedication to all that you do. Lastly, thank you for bringing me on this journey with you; it has been a good learning experience and I am better for it.

I would also echo the words of Carolyn by thanking the Chalice Press team. To Brad Lyons, Deb Arca, Gail Stobaugh, Hui Chu Wang, and our editor Ulrike Guthrie "thank you" for the work all of you have put into bringing this project to fruition! Thank you does not seem adequate. Grace and peace to you all.

Finally, I would like to thank my husband, Leon, and my children (Asa and Eden). There is nothing like having to live what you teach and preach in front of those who see you the most. These three people keep me honest, remind me of what is important in this life, and challenge me to be the best version of myself. They are my family—they are home. Thank you for giving me space to participate in this work.

Appendix A

About the Authors—Autobiographies of Culture

When any single person enters into conversation with someone else, these two people bring with them the cultures they inhabit. But each person lives and operates within his or her own cultural habits, formed by personal histories and experiences of living in different communities. As children grow, parents may see cultural shifts when a child moves from elementary to middle school. Different classmates and learning environments can create new cultural atmospheres, and each person adapts and learns from those atmospheres in his or her own way.

We authors have come from our own particular cultural backgrounds, and our individual histories and contexts have shaped who we are. One of the tasks we wanted to accomplish in this book was to model the kind of cultural excavation we can each do on our own lives, listening to our own histories and uniqueness, and sharing that with one another. So in this section, we share our own cultural autobiographies with you.

We hope they will serve as jumping-off points for defining your own autobiography of identity and culture. As you read through each of ours, consider the major milestones in your own life that have formed parts of your identity. Reflect on the ways you have been exposed to differences along your journey and how learning about those different cultures and experiences have impacted you. Writing your own autobiography of culture can help you reconnect with aspects of your heritage and deepen your appreciation for the influences of others along the way.

Joy Shares: Cultural Adjustments From Germany to North Carolina to New York

I (Y. Joy Harris-Smith) spent the majority of my growing up in Queens, New York. However, before New York we lived in Germany, where I was born. My father was in the United States Air Force.

When our family returned to the United States, I was about three years old and we lived in North Carolina, on a military base and off, before eventually moving to Queens.

My family, during my early years, was a middle-class black family who had achieved the American dream. My father worked outside the home, and my mother stayed at home to work taking care of the children. This was the life that my parents had been taught by their respective families and society to have. So life was good. We attended a Pentecostal church, and my mother was my first Sunday school teacher. During our time in North Carolina, our social and religious circles were predominately white, and honestly, I did not think much of it then—and still do not. I would like to believe the adults that surrounded me in these familial and religious spaces knew how to honor the similarities and respect the differences—my memories from that time, most of them, are happy ones. Yet before leaving rural North Carolina I saw something that would resurface over and over as I made a new life in New York.

One day my mom needed to go and get gas for the car. Now if you know anything about living in rural places, sometimes a drive to the gas station becomes a trip, at least for the kids, because the drive was not a short distance. After my mom got the gas and was making the U-turn at the partition in the road, I saw three people on the side of the road. Two of the people were obviously male and dressed in military fatigues, and the third person was dressed in a Ku Klux Klan outfit. The sign he was holding said, "White Men Only." I'm not sure how I knew what the person in white represented, but I did, and I could read the sign. As I opened my mouth, my mother immediately hushed me and stepped on the gas. I remember her saying to me to not tell anyone at church what we had seen. I didn't understand then why she would say this, but I have some educated guesses now as to why she gave this instruction. This was my introduction, my preamble, to race.

My transition from the South to the North was an interesting one. For me, it was definitely a lot more apparent how distinct the regional differences were. There was teasing, mostly from family members, of my thick Southern drawl, which Northerners often mistake for lack of intelligence. There was blacktop in the back of the school yard, and I was most certainly used to grass, open fields, and the woods. Even in New York I still had a love of playing outside and being in the elements. In New York there were cold winters, in which I learned to don leg warmers before my mother realized it was time—and okay—for me to wear pants, but not until about the fifth or sixth grade. These were cultural and even some religious differences that I learned to engage, adjusting to life in a big city. Race played a part too. There was a shift in who my friends and classmates were, in part because of where I lived. In North Carolina most of my friends and classmates were white, and when I moved to New York most of my friends and classmates were black. New York City is a great place, but I learned it also is a segregated one. I will explain more about this later.

The rest of my formative years in Queens were spent in church, at school, and around extended family. Summers were characterized by camps and games of kickball and baseball with the kids in my Springfield Gardens neighborhood. Both of my parents came from musically gifted families, so I began taking clarinet lessons in the fourth grade, sang in the chorus throughout middle school, and joined the junior choir at church with a stint in St. Claire's marching band playing the fife. This was a Catholic school that my sixth grade social studies teacher taught at and asked us to consider joining. With our mother's permission all three of us—me and my two brothers—made it a family affair. I also took a couple of years of piano lessons—a family tradition. In addition to music, I also gained much practice with speaking publicly, at church for the holidays with Easter and Christmas recitations and in the storytelling contest I won in the fifth grade.

Even though the middle school I attended was predominately black in a predominately black neighborhood, the fact that there were cultural differences even among black people had not registered with me before. However, some of my classmates were well aware of this—and they educated me. Their parents were from places such as Jamaica, Barbados, Guyana, Haiti, and Bermuda. Going to high school in Brooklyn, N.Y. for a semester helped to bring some additional clarity between these ethnic/cultural groups. The commute from Brooklyn to Queens proved to be a bit much for me, and happily my mother helped me transfer back to a high school in the neighborhood. I came back to a very ethnically diverse high school in Queens. Indian, Indo-Caribbean, African American, Caribbean Black, White, and African students—high school was a melting pot, at least in most of the classes that I took. My teachers were White, Black, Asian, and Hispanic. My big inner city high school world reflected the world we currently inhabit today.

For my college years, I longed for less crowded halls than those of my high school. I realized I wanted and needed to be in a smaller environment. I attended a small private liberal arts college in the Finger Lakes region of New York. I was the first person in my immediate family to attend college. My mother was beyond proud, happy that she lived to see that moment. During my senior year of college I lived in Senegal, West Africa. This experience caused me to do a lot of critical self-reflection. All that I had learned up till that moment was up for redefinition. I began to consider and reconsider aspects of my life: what it meant to be an American, what it meant to be a Christian, what it meant to be black, and most importantly, what it meant to be human. What kind of human did I want to be? These were some of the reflections I would take with me into the classroom as I trained to become a teacher and eventually to seminary.

Seminary was an interesting place because it was the first time I learned, in a more academic fashion, about my faith. I came from a Pentecostal background, and so academics and faith—at least for most of my life—were two separate enterprises. It was during my time in seminary that I began to understand anew the complex interconnectedness of life, culture, faith, and the academy. Since I had been abroad before, I knew I wanted to go again. So while in seminary I spent a summer in the Dominican Republic. This experience, along with my time in Dakar, reminded me of the similarities and the differences of human culture no matter where one is in the world. There are some basics to human life that can be intellectually understood yet when you see them in action, it is different. It is more palpable—tangible.

What I found most impactful is that in many of the countries I have visited as an adult, I seem to resemble the people. What I mean is that if I did not speak English in Dakar or in Santo Domingo—and depending how I wore my hair—I could be mistaken for a local. All during my education in the United States I learned about passing for white. It was amazing to me that in these other countries I could pass—not for white—but for whatever the local culture was. My skin complexion did not make me stand out because it was the norm—it was the standard.

Education, coupled with opportunities to experience and learn about people in the world, has continued to drive me toward a belief that if we would *honor the similarities* and *respect the differences,* we might find ourselves further along on this human journey.

My life and educational experiences inspired me to complete a doctoral degree in Communication and Culture. I have been challenged to live both personally and professionally the mantra of honoring the similarities and respecting the differences—from being married to someone who is from another culture to teaching at an institution where most of my students do not look like me. It has been through my work as a teacher and my travels that I am constantly reminded that we all belong to the human family—and it is this we cannot, we must not forget.

Carolyn Shares: Cultural Sampling from Across the Country

I (Carolyn Helsel) grew up in San Antonio, Texas, as part of a big family living in a predominantly white neighborhood. We were middle-class, and we attended a large downtown church on Sundays where once or twice a year I had the opportunity to make and bring breakfast to homeless persons under a nearby freeway. San Antonio has a rich cultural heritage from Mexicans and Native Americans, and my comfort food was (and still is) a good plate of refried beans, Spanish rice, and soft chicken tacos. Many of us learned Spanish in middle school and high school, and as part of my church youth group, I traveled to Mexico and Costa Rica for service/learning trips. In high school, in addition to learning Spanish, I took two years of American Sign Language. I had the opportunity to learn more about deaf culture in San Antonio when our teacher Linda Anderson arranged for us to go bowling with a deaf bowling league.

For college, I traveled to Washington State and became part of a mostly white evangelical Christian college campus, where the culture of faith permeated the classrooms and the dorms. At that school, 13 percent of the student population came from Hawaii, so I learned from my peers about Hawaiian culture by taking classes on hula dancing and attending their annual Luau.

In addition to learning about other cultures, I was able to reflect on the differences between the culture I came from and the culture I found myself in while at college. From that distance, the culture of my neighborhood and school in San Antonio now seemed much more invested in outward appearances: makeup and clothes, the right accessories, a friendly smile and warm "Hel-loooo." As a college student, seeing the culture of the Pacific Northwesterners in stereotypical flannel and jeans, I realized that different parts of the country and different groups within those regions had different expectations and cultural norms. Everything in Washington seemed casual; everything in Texas seemed dressy. I was forming ideas of cultural differences—which can become stereotypes when left unquestioned.

After college, I attended graduate school in a wealthy college town in New Jersey. Here were new cultural experiences: more regional differences among students, more international students, more opportunities to learn from persons with different beliefs and political views, and more intergenerational social interactions since many of my classmates were second-career students. I also began learning more about the histories of the women's and civil rights movements, discovering from course readings and classmates' sharing that racism was still alive and well. This would later fuel my interest in studying communication with white churches to help them talk about racism.

Until seminary, I had not realized the cultural differences associated with being a *white Christian*. I had not consciously thought of myself as white or part of a larger white Christian culture, but once in seminary I was beginning to notice more of the differences not only between different kinds of Christian faith and practice among Christians more generally, but among *white* Christians specifically. Since then I have learned the quote from Delores Williams, who recalls her grandmother—the daughter of slaves—telling her: "White folks and us are both Christian, but we ain't got the same religion."[1] There are different cultural expressions within different worshiping communities—and I had not realized how the history of racism had impacted these differences.

I also had not realized that white Christians had cultural differences too: different ways of being a Christian based not only on denominations, but on whether you considered yourself an "evangelical" or "liberal," or even sought to combine the two as a "progressive evangelical." Since that time, after becoming aware of the pain inflicted by many evangelicals—supposedly people who want to share "good news," but who condemn persons for loving someone of the same gender or reject women who feel called by God to preach—I have distanced myself from that label.

And yet I still struggle with whether or not I identify as some kind of "evangelical." I indeed believe there to be good news that my religious tradition has to share with others: that Jesus challenged political and social systems that denied persons full dignity, and that the resurrected Christ speaks to God's perpetual "no" to the powers of death we continue to inflict on one another. And I know many evangelicals who are working to bring greater attention to issues of social justice, particularly racism. This part of my identity struggle goes on—I continue to try to discern who I am as a person

---

[1]Watch Williams's whole speech at the 2002 Women Clergy Conference at Harvard Divinity School here: https://www.youtube.com/watch?v=hltJgzbXPFI. She reads this line at minute 12:19.

of deep religious faith who wants to help others find their preaching voice for proclaiming good news.

I met my husband in seminary, and the two of us moved to Yuma, Arizona, after seminary to work in a hospital as chaplains. While we were there, we cared for families after the deaths of patients, and along the way, I noticed how different groups of people were treated differently by staff. For instance, there were differences in staffs' expectations of which groups would be more "disruptive" in their grief responses. They tended to expect Native American families to be more reserved in their expressions of grief, but regularly called on chaplains to respond when families of Latinx patients grieved, expecting the latter group to be more vocal and perhaps disruptive to other patients. In this experience, I saw cultural stereotypes and learned how our expectations are often wrong. First, when anyone dies, it is natural for us to mourn, and being allowed to make loud expressions of grief should be the right of anyone who has lost a loved one. Second, we may have stereotypes about who is more comfortable with expressing emotion, and we need to be open to challenging those stereotypes.

I accompanied a Native American family through the dying process as a loved one got sicker in the hospital and eventually had to be taken off life support, and I witnessed the loud wailing and sobs of the family in mourning. I participated in their death rituals that later took place on the reservation, a two-day event accompanied by more loud cries as they walked the casket into the Cry House and later burned the casket on a funeral pyre with clothing made especially for this mourning ritual. It was a powerful event, and it felt like a privilege for me to be able to attend.

After a year, we moved to San Antonio (back to my hometown) when my husband and I got jobs in the area. He worked with hospice and I at a local church, where members mostly came from military families. Working with men and women and youth who were connected in some way to our nation's armed forces educated me about another kind of culture: people from different races and ethnicities who share similar values of patriotism and loyalty, as well as a comfort and respect for a variety of cultural differences, since many had moved around during their years of service.

The congregants at my first church who had served in the military taught me a great deal. I met women in their eighties who had served as high-ranking officers long before women had access to high-ranking positions in the corporate sector. I met a man who shared of his experience as a prisoner of war in an Asian country, who later married an Asian woman—his negative experiences as a prisoner of war not prejudicing him against others who shared in some cultural similarities. Many persons who had served in the military had much more familiarity with different cultures and races than others from the same community they lived in currently.

After San Antonio, we moved back to Princeton, where I worked as associate director of admissions for Princeton Seminary. I had the opportunity to learn from some amazing applicants who shared with me some of their life stories. I also got to know better the Italian Catholic cultural heritage of many of my white colleagues— staff who worked in the admissions office and who commuted into Princeton from Pennsylvania or other parts of New Jersey.

Our family lived in Atlanta for two years while I worked on my Ph.D. at Emory University, and I encountered the rich cultural heritage of African Americans living in the South, continuing to experience racism yet resisting on multiple levels the oppression that met them at every turn. I learned from one of our friends about Korean American culture; as a divorced first-generation mother of two, she experienced subtle and overt racism from the white church where she served, as well as disdain from the Korean community because of her status as a divorcee.

While in Atlanta, I also lived as a poor doctoral student, with two young children, as my husband also worked on his Ph.D. We received WIC benefits that helped us pay bills for food while we both studied and taught and raised our kids. I went to a welfare office where I had to fill out paperwork and have my blood drawn, and talk to nutritionists about how I was feeding my baby in order to receive the vouchers that would allow me to get free cheese, milk, and cans of beans at the grocery store. In line at the store, when I would pay with these vouchers, I felt awkward glances from other customers and from store clerks when they had to explain to me that I had picked up the wrong size of cheese and that the voucher would only pay for the other size, so I would have to go back. It was a cultural experience that taught me that our society makes it very difficult for the poor to receive social services, and those who do receive them are likely to be shamed for it.

Once my husband got a job, we moved our family to the greater Boston area, where he commuted into the city to teach several times a week. We had only one car for a while, so I would often feel stranded at home with two kids. In order to get out, I would take them on walks in the neighborhood. I noticed that greeting people on the sidewalk with a friendly smile or warm "Good mornin'" was not typically well-received. In fact, my comments would often go ignored, my friendly glances not returned. I discovered that cultural practices in New England were different yet again from the cultures of other regions where I had lived. People who did not know you were not willing to make eye contact on the street. But people were still friendly once you got to know them and they had a reason to trust you. It is much like the winters in the Boston area—long and cold, but beautiful when the weather eventually warms up.

I also discovered in Boston that white people were glad I was doing research on racism, but they felt the real audience for my work would be southerners. I began to realize why there is a historic sense of conflict between the North and the South; white northerners assumed they already "got it" when it came to race and that they have always been on the right side, oblivious to the ongoing challenges of addressing racism in the North. The history of bussing in Boston revealed a particularly painful episode of backlash to racial integration.

After three years, our family moved to Austin, Texas, when I got a job teaching at a seminary. It was not until recently that I realized how familiar so much of the culture feels to me, and I realize that it puts me at a great advantage. I have a sense of comfort that escapes many persons who feel more like outsiders in Texas. I recently sat with a group of moms who had all immigrated to the United States from elsewhere: Spain, Australia, South Africa, and France. Although most of these moms were white and had the privileges associated with whiteness, they all felt out of step with the culture around them, isolated and worried about how to raise their own children in a culture different from their own.

Back in Texas, I also have more opportunities to reconnect with people I knew while growing up here, and I am realizing there are many ways that our similarities have ended with our upbringing. Many have political views formed by other media outlets than the ones I view, perspectives on race and immigration that approach current conflicts very differently, and ideas around human sexuality that are very different from mine. We grew up in the same "culture," but we are now each part of very different and separate cultures.

I am also finding many more diverse voices here in Austin, and from people I went to high school with, now that I have been on this journey. Friends of mine who were "in the closet" have come out as gay in their adulthood. People in my neighborhood come from places all over the world: Scotland, Mexico, Nigeria, India. I am learning about cultural differences every day and loving it. I am still on this journey of understanding my own cultural backgrounds and how my identity shapes who I am, and also how my identity gets shaped by the amazing people I get to meet along the way.

Appendix B

Books to Read to Develop Greater Empathy

Picture Books

— *1001 Inventions and Awesome Facts from Muslim Civilization: Official Children's Companion to the 1001 Inventions Exhibition* by National Geographic (Islam)

— *ABC A Family Alphabet Book* by Bobbie Combs (different families)

— *All Are Welcome* by Alexandra Penfold (school classroom where all are welcome)

— *A Moon for Moe and Mo* by Jane Breskin Zalben (Jewish and Muslim boys become friends)

— *And Tango Makes Three* by Justin Richardson and Peter Parnell (two penguin dads)

— *And That's Why She's My Mama* by Tiarra Nizario (adoption)

— *El Chupacabras* by Adam Rubin (bi-lingual English and Spanish)

— *The Colors of Us* by Karen Katz (the varieties of beautiful skin tones)

— *The Day You Begin* by Jacqueline Woodson (a child of color in a mostly white space)

— *Game Changers: The Story of Venus and Serena Williams* by Lesa Cline-Ramsome (powerful black women role models being the best in tennis)

— *Golden Domes and Silver Lanterns: A Muslim Book of Colors* by Hena Khan (Islam)

— *I Am Jazz* by Jessica Herthel and Jazz Jennings (a transgender child's perspective)

— *Julián Is a Mermaid* by Jessica Love (a boy who wants to dress up like a mermaid).

— *Mufaro's Beautiful Daughters: An African Tale* by John Steptoe (African folk tale)

— *Mommy, Mama, and Me* by Lesléa Newman (two moms)

— *The Name Jar* by Yangsook Choi (a Korean girl hides her name then celebrates it)

— *Pink Is for Boys* by Robb Pearlman (girls and boys can like the same things)

— *Princess Princess Ever After* by Katie O'Neill (two princesses fall in love)

— *Red: A Crayon's Story* by Michael Hall (a blue crayon in a red wrapper)

— *Stonewall: A Building. An Uprising. A Revolution.* by Rob Sanders (LGBTQ history)

— *Under My Hijab* by Hena Khan (Muslim women)

— *We Belong Together: A Book About Adoption and Families* by Todd Parr

— *What Does It Mean to Be an Entrepreneur?* by Rana DiOrio and Emma D. Dryden (a black girl builds a solution for a problem she sees, demonstrating being an entrepreneur)

— *Whoever You Are* by Mem Fox (beautiful pictures of children around the world sharing the same joy and pain, smiles and tears, even while their lives and homes are different)

— *Who Is My Neighbor?* By Amy-Jill Levine and Sandy Eisenberg Sasso (Jewish and Christian relations)

Nonfiction Resource Books for Older Children

— *Black Lives Matter* by Sue Bradford Edwards and Duchess Harris

— *The Civil Rights Movement* by Irma McClaurin with Virginia Schomp

— *The Harlem Renaissance* by Dolores Johnson with Virginia Schomp

— *Pride: Celebrating Diversity and Community* by Robin Stevenson

— *Taking Action Against Racism* by Cath Senker

Middle-Grade Chapter Books and Graphic Novels (with synopses from Amazon.com)

— *American Born Chinese* by Gene Luen Yang

Synopsis: Jin Wang starts at a new school where he's the only Chinese-American student. When a boy from Taiwan joins his class, Jin doesn't want to be associated with an FOB [Fresh Off the Boat— an immigrant who just recently came to this country] like him. Jin just wants to be an all-American boy, because he's in love with an all-American girl. Danny is an all-American boy: great at basketball, popular with the girls. But his obnoxious Chinese cousin Chin-Kee's annual visit is such a disaster that it ruins Danny's reputation at school, leaving him with no choice but to transfer somewhere he can start all over again. The Monkey King has lived for thousands of years and mastered the arts of kung fu and the heavenly disciplines. He's ready to join the ranks of the immortal gods in heaven. But there's no place in heaven for a monkey. Each of these characters cannot help himself alone, but how can they possibly help each other? They're going to have to find a way if they want fix the disasters their lives have become.

— *Amina's Voice* by Hena Khan

Synopsis: Amina has never been comfortable in the spotlight. She is happy just hanging out with her best friend, Soojin. Except now that she's in middle school everything feels different. Soojin is suddenly hanging out with Emily, one of the "cool" girls in the class, and even talking about changing her name to something more "American." Does Amina need to start changing too? Or hiding who she is to fit in? While Amina grapples with these questions, she is devastated when her local mosque is vandalized.

Amina's Voice brings to life the joys and challenges of a young Pakistani-American and highlights the many ways in which one girl's voice can help bring a diverse community together to love and support each other.

— *As the Crow Flies* by Melanie Gillman

Synopsis: Charlie Lamonte is thirteen years old, queer, black, and questioning what was once a firm belief in God. So naturally, she's spending a week of her summer vacation stuck at an all-white Christian youth backpacking camp. As the journey wears on and the rhetoric wears thin, she can't help but poke holes in the pious obliviousness of this storied sanctuary with little regard for people like herself... or her fellow camper, Sydney.

— *Being Jazz: My Life as a (Transgender) Teen* by Jazz Jennings

Synopsis: Jazz Jennings is one of the youngest and most prominent voices in the national discussion about gender identity. At the age of five, Jazz transitioned to life as a girl, with the support of her parents. A year later, her parents allowed her to share her incredible journey in her first Barbara Walters interview, aired at a time when the public was much less knowledgeable or accepting of the transgender community. This groundbreaking interview was followed over the years by other high-profile interviews, a documentary, the launch of her YouTube channel, a picture book, and her own reality TV series—I Am Jazz—making her one of the most recognizable activists for transgender teens, children, and adults.

In her remarkable memoir, Jazz reflects on these very public experiences and how they have helped shape the mainstream attitude toward the transgender community. But it hasn't all been easy. Jazz has faced many challenges, bullying, discrimination, and rejection, yet she perseveres as she educates others about her life as a transgender teen. Through it all, her family has been beside her on this journey, standing together against those who don't understand the true meaning of tolerance and unconditional love. Now Jazz must learn to navigate the physical, social, and emotional upheavals of adolescence—particularly high school—complicated by the unique challenges of being a transgender teen. Making the journey from girl to woman is never easy—especially when you began your life in a boy's body."

— *Blended* by Sharon M. Draper

Synopsis: Eleven-year-old Isabella's parents are divorced, so she has to switch lives every week: One week she's Isabella with her dad, his girlfriend Anastasia, and Anastasia's son Darren living in a fancy house where they are one of the only black families in the neighborhood. The next week she's Izzy with her mom and her boyfriend John-Mark in a small, not-so-fancy house that she loves.

Because of this, Isabella has always felt pulled between two worlds. And now that her parents are divorced, it seems their fights are even worse, and they're always about HER. Isabella feels even more stuck in the middle, split and divided between them than ever. And she's is beginning to realize that being split between Mom and Dad is more than switching houses, switching nicknames, switching backpacks: it's also about switching identities. Her dad is black, her mom is white, and strangers are always commenting: "You're so exotic!" "You look so unusual." "But what are you really?" She knows what they're really saying: "You don't look like your parents." "You're different." "What race are you really?" And when her parents, who both get engaged [again] at the same time, get in their biggest fight ever, Isabella doesn't just feel divided, she feels ripped in two. What does it mean to be half white or half black? To belong to half mom and half dad? And if you're only seen as half of this and half of that, how can you ever feel whole?

It seems like nothing can bring Isabella's family together again—until the worst happens. Isabella and Darren are stopped by the police. A cell phone is mistaken for a gun. And shots are fired.

— *Bud, Not Buddy* by Christopher Paul Curtis

Synopsis: It's 1936, in Flint, Michigan. Times may be hard, and ten-year-old Bud may be a motherless boy on the run, but Bud's got a few things going for him:

1. He has his own suitcase full of special things.

2. He's the author of *Bud Caldwell's Rules and Things for Having a Funner Life and Making a Better Liar Out of Yourself.*

3. His momma never told him who his father was, but she left a clue: flyers advertising Herman E. Calloway and his famous band, the Dusky Devastators of the Depression!!!!!!

Bud's got an idea that those flyers will lead him to his father. Once he decides to hit the road to find this mystery man, nothing can stop him—not hunger, not fear, not vampires, not even Herman E. Calloway himself.

— *The Crossover* by Kwame Alexander

Synopsis: "With a bolt of lightning on my kicks...The court is SIZZLING. My sweat is DRIZZLING. Stop all that quivering. 'Cuz tonight I'm delivering," raps twelve-year-old Josh Bell. Thanks to their dad, Josh and his twin brother, Jordan, are kings on the court. But Josh has more than basketball in his blood—he's got mad beats, too, which help him find his rhythm when it's all on the line.

As their winning season unfolds, things begin to change. When Jordan meets a girl, the twins' bond unravels. Told in dynamic verse, this fast and furious middle grade novel that started it all absolutely bounces with rhythm and bursts with heart.

— *Drum Roll, Please* by Lisa Jenn Bigelow

Synopsis: Melly only joined the school band because her best friend, Olivia, begged her to. But to her surprise, quiet Melly loves playing the drums. It's the only time she doesn't feel like a mouse. Now she and Olivia are about to spend the next two weeks at Camp Rockaway, jamming under the stars in the Michigan woods.

But this summer brings a lot of big changes for Melly: her parents split up, her best friend ditches her, and Melly finds herself unexpectedly falling for another girl at camp. To top it all off, Melly's not sure she has what it takes to be a real rock n' roll drummer. Will she be able to make music from all the noise in her heart?

— *Echo* by Pam Muñoz Ryan

Synopsis: Lost and alone in a forbidden forest, Otto meets three mysterious sisters and suddenly finds himself entwined in a puzzling quest involving a prophecy, a promise, and a harmonica.

Decades later, Friedrich in Germany, Mike in Pennsylvania, and Ivy in California each, in turn, become interwoven when the very same harmonica lands in their lives. All the children face daunting challenges: rescuing a father, protecting a brother, holding a family together. And ultimately, pulled by the invisible thread of destiny, their suspenseful solo stories converge in an orchestral crescendo.

Richly imagined and masterfully crafted, *Echo* pushes the boundaries of genre, form, and storytelling innovation to create a wholly original novel that will resound in your heart long after the last note has been struck.

— *El Deafo* by Cece Bell

Synopsis: Going to school and making new friends can be tough. But going to school and making new friends while wearing a bulky hearing aid strapped to your chest? That requires superpowers! In this funny, poignant graphic novel memoir, author/illustrator Cece Bell chronicles her hearing loss at a young age and her subsequent experiences with the Phonic Ear, a very powerful—and very awkward—hearing aid. The Phonic Ear gives Cece the ability to hear—sometimes things she shouldn't—but also isolates her from her classmates. She really just wants to fit in and find a true friend, someone who appreciates her as she is. After some trouble, she is finally able to harness the power of the Phonic Ear and become "El Deafo, Listener for All." And more importantly, declare a place for herself in the world and find the friend she's longed for.

— *Esperanza Rising* by Pam Muñoz Ryan

Synopsis: Esperanza thought she'd always live a privileged life on her family's ranch in Mexico. She'd always have fancy dresses, a beautiful home filled with servants, and Mama, Papa, and Abuelita to care for her. But a sudden tragedy forces Esperanza and Mama to flee to California and settle in a Mexican farm labor camp. Esperanza isn't ready for the hard work, financial struggles brought on by the Great Depression, or lack of acceptance she now faces. When Mama gets sick and a strike for better working conditions threatens to uproot their new life, Esperanza must find a way to rise above her difficult circumstances—because Mama's life, and her own, depend on it.

— *George* by Alex Gino

Synopsis: When people look at George, they think they see a boy. But she knows she's not a boy. She knows she's a girl

George thinks she'll have to keep this a secret forever. Then her teacher announces that their class play is going to be *Charlotte's Web*. George really, really, REALLY wants to play Charlotte. But the teacher says she can't even try out for the part...because she's a boy.

With the help of her best friend, Kelly, George comes up with a plan. Not just so she can be Charlotte—but so everyone can know who she is, once and for all.

— *Ghost Boys* by Jewell Parker Rhodes

Synopsis: *Only the living can make the world better. Live and make it better.*

Twelve-year-old Jerome is shot by a police officer who mistakes his toy gun for a real threat. As a ghost, he observes the devastation that's been unleashed on his family and community in the wake of what they see as an unjust and brutal killing.

Soon Jerome meets another ghost: Emmett Till, a boy from a very different time but similar circumstances. Emmett helps Jerome process what has happened, on a journey towards recognizing how historical racism may have led to the events that ended his life. Jerome also meets Sarah, the daughter of the police officer, who grapples with her father's actions.

Once again Jewell Parker Rhodes deftly weaves historical and sociopolitical layers into a gripping and poignant story about how children and families face the complexities of today's world, and how one boy grows to understand American blackness in the aftermath of his own death.

— *Harbor Me* by Jacqueline Woodson

Synopsis: It all starts when six kids have to meet for a weekly chat—by themselves, with no adults to listen in. There, in the room they soon dub it the ARTT Room (short for "A Room to Talk"), they discover it's safe to talk about what's bothering them—everything from Esteban's father's deportation and Haley's father's incarceration to Amari's fears of racial profiling and Ashton's adjustment to his changing family fortunes. When the six are together, they can express the feelings and fears they have to hide from the rest of the world. And together, they can grow braver and more ready for the rest of their lives.

— *Kira-Kira* by Cynthia Kadohata

Synopsis: kira-kira (kee ra kee ra): glittering; shining.

Glittering. That's how Katie Takeshima's sister, Lynn, makes everything seem. The sky is *kira-kira* because its color is deep but see-through at the same time. The sea is *kira-kira* for the same reason. And so are people's eyes. When Katie and her family move from a Japanese community in Iowa to the Deep South of Georgia, it's Lynn who explains to her why people stop on the street to stare. And it's Lynn who, with her special way of viewing the world, teaches Katie to look beyond tomorrow. But when Lynn becomes desperately ill, and the whole family begins to fall apart, it is up to Katie to find a way to remind them all that there is always something glittering—*kira-kira*—in the future.

— *A Long Walk to Water: Based on a True Story* by Linda Sue Park

Synopsis: The *New York Times* bestseller *A Long Walk to Water* begins as two stories, told in alternating sections, about two eleven-year-olds in Sudan, a girl in 2008 and a boy in 1985. The girl, Nya, is fetching water from a pond that is two hours' walk from her home: she makes two trips to the pond every day. The boy, Salva, becomes one of the "lost boys" of Sudan, refugees who cover the African continent on foot as they search for their families and for a safe place to stay. Enduring every hardship from loneliness to attack by armed rebels to contact with killer lions and crocodiles, Salva is a survivor, and his story goes on to intersect with Nya's in an astonishing and moving way.

— *Number the Stars* by Lois Lowry

Synopsis: As the German troops begin their campaign to "relocate" all the Jews of Denmark, Annemarie Johansen's family takes in Annemarie's best friend, Ellen Rosen, and conceals her as part of the family.

Through the eyes of ten-year-old Annemarie, we watch as the Danish Resistance smuggles almost the entire Jewish population of Denmark, nearly seven thousand people, across the sea to Sweden. The heroism of an entire nation reminds us that there was pride and human decency in the world even during a time of terror and war.

— *Out of My Mind* by Sharon M. Draper

Synopsis: From multiple award-winning author Sharon Draper comes a story that will forever change how we all look at anyone with a disability, perfect for fans of R. J. Palacio's *Wonder*.

Eleven-year-old Melody is not like most people. She can't walk. She can't talk. She can't write. All because she has cerebral palsy. But she also has a photographic memory; she can remember every detail of everything she has ever experienced. She's the smartest kid in her whole school, but NO ONE knows it. Most people— her teachers, her doctors, her classmates—dismiss her as mentally challenged because she can't tell them otherwise. But Melody refuses to be defined by her disability. And she's determined to let everyone know it...somehow.

— *Pashmina* by Nidhi Chanani

Synopsis: Priyanka Das has so many unanswered questions: Why did her mother abandon her home in India years ago? What was it like there? And most importantly, who is her father, and why did her mom leave him behind? But Pri's mom avoids these questions the topic of India is permanently closed.

For Pri, her mother's homeland can only exist in her imagination. That is, until she finds a mysterious pashmina tucked away in a forgotten suitcase. When she wraps herself in it, she is transported to a place more vivid and colorful than any guidebook or Bollywood film. But is this the real India? And what is that shadow lurking in the background? To learn the truth, Pri must travel farther than she's ever dared and find the family she never knew.

In this heartwarming graphic novel debut, Nidhi Chanani weaves a tale about the hardship and self-discovery that is born from juggling two cultures and two worlds.

— *Rebound* by Kwame Alexander

Synopsis: Before Josh and Jordan Bell were streaking up and down the court, their father was learning his own moves. In this prequel to Newbery Medal winner *The Crossover,* Chuck Bell takes center stage, as readers get a glimpse of his childhood and how he became the jazz music worshiping, basketball star his sons look up to.

A novel in verse with all the impact and rhythm readers have come to expect from Kwame Alexander, *Rebound* will go back in time to visit the childhood of Chuck "Da Man" Bell during one pivotal summer when young Charlie is sent to stay with his grandparents where he discovers basketball and learns more about his family's past.

— *Roll of Thunder, Hear My Cry* by Mildred D. Taylor

Synopsis: Set in Mississippi at the height of the Depression, this is the story of one family's struggle to maintain their integrity, pride, and independence in the face of racism and social injustice. And it is also Cassie's story—Cassie Logan, an independent girl who discovers over the course of an important year why having land of their own is so crucial to the Logan family, even as she learns to draw strength from her own sense of dignity and self-respect.

— *Star Crossed* by Barbara Dee

Synopsis: Twelve-year-old Mattie is thrilled when she learns the eighth grade play will be *Romeo and Juliet*. In particular, she can't wait to share the stage with Gemma Braithwaite, who has been cast as Juliet. Gemma is brilliant, pretty—and British!—and Mattie starts to see her as more than just a friend. But Mattie has also had an on/

off crush on her classmate Elijah since, well, *forever*. Is it possible to have a crush on both boys AND girls?

If that wasn't enough to deal with, things offstage are beginning to resemble their own Shakespearean drama: the cast is fighting, and the boy playing Romeo may not be up to the challenge of the role. And due to a last-minute emergency, Mattie is asked to step up and take over the leading role—opposite Gemma's Juliet—just as Mattie's secret crush starts to become not-so-secret in her group of friends.

— *Underground Abductor: An Abolitionist Tale about Harriet Tubman* by Nathan Hale

Synopsis: Araminta Ross was born a slave in Delaware in the early nineteenth century. Slavery meant that her family could be ripped apart at any time, and that she could be put to work in dangerous places and for abusive people. But north of the Mason-Dixon line, slavery was illegal. If she could run away and make it north without being caught or killed, she'd be free. Facing enormous danger, Araminta made it, and once free, she changed her name to Harriet Tubman. Tubman spent the rest of her life helping slaves run away like she did, every time taking her life in her hands. Nathan Hale tells her incredible true-life story with the humor and sensitivity he's shown in every one of the Hazardous Tales—perfect for reluctant readers and classroom discussions.

— *Yes, I'm Hot in This: The Hilarious Truth about Life in a Hijab* by Huda Fahmy

Synopsis: At some point in our lives, we've all felt a little out of place. Huda Fahmy has found it's a little more difficult to fade into the crowd when wearing a hijab.

In *Yes, I'm Hot in This*, Huda navigates the sometimes-rocky waters of life from the unique perspective of an American-Muslim woman, breaking down misconceptions of her culture one comic at a time. From recounting the many questions she gets about her hijab every day (yes, she *does* have hair) and explaining how she runs in an abaya (just fine, thank you) to dealing with misconceptions about Muslims, *Yes, I'm Hot in This* tackles universal feelings from a point of view we don't hear from nearly enough.

Every one of us has experienced love, misunderstanding, anger, and a deep desire for pizza. In *Yes, I'm Hot in This,* Huda's clever comics demonstrate humor's ability to bring us together, no matter how different we may appear on the surface.

Books for Older Teens and Young Adult Novels (with synopses from Amazon.com)

— *The Hate U Give* by Angie Thomas

Synopsis: Sixteen-year-old Starr Carter moves between two worlds: the poor neighborhood where she lives and the fancy suburban prep school she attends. The uneasy balance between these worlds is shattered when Starr witnesses the fatal shooting of her childhood best friend Khalil at the hands of a police officer. Khalil was unarmed.

Soon afterward, his death is a national headline. Some are calling him a thug, maybe even a drug dealer and a gangbanger. Protesters are taking to the streets in Khalil's name. Some cops and the local drug lord try to intimidate Starr and her family. What everyone wants to know is: what *really* went down that night? And the only person alive who can answer that is Starr. But what Starr does—or does not—say could upend her community. It could also endanger her life.

— *On the Come Up* by Angie Thomas

Synopsis: Sixteen-year-old Bri wants to be one of the greatest rappers of all time. Or at least win her first battle. As the daughter of an underground hip hop legend who died right before he hit big, Bri's got massive shoes to fill.

But it's hard to get your come up when you're labeled a hoodlum at school, and your fridge at home is empty after your mom loses her job. So Bri pours her anger and frustration into her first song, which goes viral...for all the wrong reasons.

Bri soon finds herself at the center of a controversy, portrayed by the media as more menace than MC. But with an eviction notice staring her family down, Bri doesn't just want to make it—she *has* to. Even if it means becoming the very thing the public has made her out to be.

Insightful, unflinching, and full of heart, *On the Come Up* is an ode to hip hop from one of the most influential literary voices of a generation. It is the story of fighting for your dreams, even as the odds are stacked against you; and about how, especially for young black people, freedom of speech isn't always free.

— *Piecing Me Together* by Renée Watson

Synopsis: Acclaimed author Renée Watson offers a powerful story about a girl striving for success in a world that too often seems like it's trying to break her.

Jade believes she must get out of her poor neighborhood if she's ever going to succeed. Her mother tells her to take advantage of every opportunity that comes her way. And Jade has: every day she rides the bus away from her friends and to the private school where she feels like an outsider, but where she has plenty of opportunities. But some *opportunities* she doesn't really welcome, like an invitation to join Women to Women, a mentorship program for "at-risk" girls. Just because her mentor is black and graduated from the same high school doesn't mean she understands where Jade is coming from. She's tired of being singled out as someone who needs help, someone people want to fix. Jade wants to speak, to create, to express her joys and sorrows, her pain and her hope. Maybe there are some things she could show other women about understanding the world and finding ways to be real, to make a difference.

— *Rethinking Normal: A Memoir in Transition* by Katie Rain Hill

Synopsis: In her unique, generous, and affecting voice, nineteen-year-old Katie Rain Hill shares her personal journey of undergoing gender reassignment. Now with a reading group guide!

Katie Rain Hill realized very young that a serious mistake had been made; she was a girl who had been born in the body of a boy.

Suffocating under her peers' bullying and the mounting pressure to be "normal," Katie tried to take her life at the age of eight years old. After several other failed attempts, she finally understood that "Katie"—the girl trapped within her—was determined to live.

In this first-person account, Katie reflects on her pain-filled childhood and the events leading up to the life-changing decision to undergo gender reassignment as a teenager. She reveals the unique challenges she faced while unlearning how to be a boy and shares what it was like to navigate the dating world—and experience heartbreak for the first time—in a body that matched her gender identity.

Told in an unwaveringly honest voice, *Rethinking Normal* is a coming-of-age story about transcending physical appearances and redefining the parameters of "normalcy" to embody one's true self.

— *Some Assembly Required: The Not-So-Secret Life of a Transgender Teen* by Arin Andrews

Synopsis: In this revolutionary first-of-its-kind memoir, Arin Andrews details the journey that led him to make the life-transforming decision to undergo gender reassignment as a high school junior. In his captivatingly witty, honest voice, Arin reveals the challenges he faced as a boy in a girl's body, the humiliation and anger he felt after getting kicked out of his private school, and all the changes—both mental and physical—he experienced once his transition began.

Some Assembly Required is a true coming-of-age story about knocking down obstacles and embracing family, friendship, and first love. But more than that, it is a reminder that self-acceptance does not come ready-made with a manual and spare parts. Rather, some assembly is always required.

Book Lists for Parents

Beyond the books cited in the main chapters of the book, these are additional resources to read and consider adopting as book club selections or buying for your own home library:

Gender and Sexuality

— *Beyond Magenta: Transgender Teens Speak Out* by Susan Kuklin

— *From the Dress-Up Corner to the Senior Prom: Navigating Gender and Sexuality Diversity in PreK–12 Schools* by Jennifer Bryan

— *The Queer and Transgender Resilience Workbook: Skills for Navigating Sexual Orientation & Gender Expression* by Anneliese A. Singh

— *Raising Ryland: Our Story of Parenting a Transgender Child with No Strings Attached* by Hillary Whittington

— *She/He/They/Me: For the Sisters, Misters, and Binary Resisters* by Robyn Ryle

— *This Is a Book for Parents of Gay Kids: A Question & Answer Guide to Everyday Life* by Dannielle Owens-Reid and Kristin Russo

— *The Transgender Child: A Handbook for Families and Professionals* by Stephanie A. Brill and Rachel Pepper

Race

— *An African American and Latinx History of the United States* by Paul Ortiz

— *An Indigenous Peoples' History of the United States* by Roxanne Dunbar-Ortiz

— *How to Be an Antiracist* by Ibram X. Kendi

— *Raising White Kids: Bringing Up Children in a Racially Unjust America* by Jennifer Harvey

— *White Rage: The Unspoken Truth of Our Racial Divide* by Carol Anderson

— *Why Are All the Black Kids Sitting Together in the Cafeteria?: And Other Conversations About Race* by Beverly Daniel Tatum

Websites

https://www.healthychildren.org/English/healthy-living/
emotional-wellness/Building-Resilience/Pages/Talking-to-
Children-About-Racial-Bias.aspx

http://www.tolerance.org/sites/default/files/general/beyond_
golden_rule.pdf

www.teacherspayteachers.com Joy notes that these are important
resources that other teachers have already made available to
one another. There is no need to reinvent the wheel. But each
curriculum lesson should also be reappropriated to make it work
in your context because each classroom is different, each group
of kids is different, and each teacher is different.

The website https://www.embracerace.org/blog/26-childrens-books
-to-support-conversations-on-race-racism-resistance   provides
updated lists of children's books that can be used in a variety of
contexts for conversations about race and racism.

Appendix C

Curriculum Activities for Teachers and Parents of Children and Youth

I. Activities for Young Children:

1. *Begin with Words Kids Can Understand: Bias and Unfairness*

A good way to begin is to discuss anti-bias education with your child's school or others in your family and how it can benefit the rest of the curriculum. For teachers, being aware of anti-bias techniques can help them be prepared to respond carefully to comments children make to one another that can lead to hurt feelings or marginalization.

Using the word "bias" may not connect with young children, so using the word "fairness" might be better. Help children understand why and in what ways your classroom can be an anti-bias space, and how this benefits all the children in the class.

For parents, you can talk as a family about what you believe about the existence of bias—what it is, what it means, and how you as a family can work against bias. Again, if the word "fairness" makes more sense, use that word when talking about it with your children.

Help children to see how issues of fairness play out not only in their home (if there are siblings, the concept of fairness may already be a contentious issue), but also in the larger society.

Help your children learn about how people can be treated unfairly because of something they cannot control, and what your children can do to speak up for others and to work against such unfairness.

This may seem overwhelming, and at times especially challenging, such as when we hear a comment we find offensive from either another parent or a child (ours or someone else's). It's good to have a game plan for what to do when this happens, because it will catch you off guard.

In responding to comments from other parents or children, begin first with taking a deep breath. Try not to react negatively or give them the cold shoulder, and instead invite them to share more about their reasoning behind their comment. Remember that each of us carries with us our own blind spots, and that some people may need you to be gentle in pointing out theirs to them.

This is especially true of young children. If you come off too strongly reprimanding them for something they have said, they will feel an abundance of shame, which does not aid in learning.

It is best to keep your own goals and values in mind. Ask yourself, Why do I want to help my child or children learn about differences? What do I want them to do and feel about their place in the world? How will I know that I have succeeded in raising up children who are comfortable with diversity and who can work against bias of many kinds?

2. Goals and Activities for Educators of Young Children

Two professional early-childhood educators, Louise Derman-Sparks and Julie Olsen Edwards, have written curriculum suggestions for anti-bias education with young children. Their goals can be a helpful starting point for us to think overall about what we want for our children. In their book, *Anti-Bias Education for Young Children and Ourselves,* Derman-Sparks and Edwards describe four goals for educating children in a way that aims to reduce bias. This is a great resource to have in your home or classroom; throughout their book, the activities they suggest for talking about different kinds of bias all support one of the four following goals:

1.   Each child will demonstrate self-awareness, confidence, family pride, and positive social identities...

2.   Each child will express comfort and joy with human diversity; accurate language for human differences; and deep, caring human connections...

3.   Each child will increasingly recognize unfairness, have language to describe unfairness, and understand that unfairness hurts...

4.   Each child will demonstrate empowerment and the skills
      to act, with others or alone, against prejudice and/or
      discriminatory actions..."[1]

These goals resonate with my own sense that shame and guilt
do not motivate persons of any age, and that instead we all need
to be able to operate from a healthy sense of who we are in order
to work effectively for social change. The first goal involves helping
all children develop a healthy sense of self, aware of their different
social identities and being able to be proud of themselves and their
families.

Another element that I think is important for engaging with
social issues is a sense of gratitude, and this echoes the second goal
above, in which children are able to approach diversity with comfort
and *joy*. We should see diversity not as a problem or something to
worry about but as a gift and an opportunity to learn more about
our world. The gifts we receive by being open to new people and
experiences can enrich our lives, and we want to communicate that
to children.

The third and fourth goals move toward naming bias and
working against it; not just celebrating diversity but recognizing
how persons are treated unfairly because of their identification as
part of a marginalized group. We want children to have the skills
to see that unfairness and feel empowered to do something about
it when they can.

Reminders for what teachers should do to increase diversity
awareness in the classroom should also include things to avoid, or
ways *not* to do it. The authors of *Anti-Bias Education* caution against
a "tourist curriculum" approach, where diversity is taught as though
children were visiting a foreign land, admiring the differences of
others in moments of holiday celebrations and traditional cuisine
without seeing the similarities and differences in everyday routines
of life, which is where cultural differences most often appear. When
we focus only on the "food, fun, and festivities" of another culture,

---

[1]Louise Derman-Sparks and Julie Olsen Edwards, *Anti-Bias Education for Young Children and Ourselves* (Washington, D.C.: National Association of Education of Young Children), 4–5.

we miss out on being able to experience the world on a daily basis through their eyes.[2] It also can lead to stereotyping persons from different cultural backgrounds, associating everyone who shares a race or ethnicity with particular traditions when each family and person individually decides how they will identify and draw from cultural resources.

Another problem with focusing on other cultures only during the holidays or focusing on cuisine alone is that the particular groups represented in that lesson may elsewhere be absent from the curriculum, and their single-day presence may give the illusion that their experiences are part of the curriculum, when in fact their experiences are actually largely absent. In choosing materials to display in the classroom, look for images that challenge stereotypes and find ways to emphasize differences and commonalities both within different groups as well as across different groups.

To enable children to see themselves represented, one task teachers can give their students is to create family portraits of everyone who lives with them, or show multiple groups of families if the parents are separated or divorced. Children can bring in their portraits and share with the rest of the class the composition of their family. This makes each child feel that their own family is considered "normal" and not different from the rest—each child comes with his or her own unique set of circumstances.

A way to introduce children to talking about skin color is by reading aloud the book *The Colors of Us* by Karen Katz.[3] This book for young readers tells the story of a young girl who notices the different shades of color in the skin of all her friends and family. The people in the story hold up their arms to one another's and compare their tones, inviting one another to discover what colors they truly see in one another. A teacher could continue this exercise in class by inviting students to put their arms together to consider the different shades of everyone's skin. What are the ways each child might describe his or her own skin tone?

---

[2]Sparks and Edwards, *Anti-Bias Education,* 8–9.
[3]Karen Katz, *The Colors of Us* (New York: Henry Holt, 1999).

Another suggestion for incorporating differences into the class is creating a project for the whole class in which students are invited to ask their parents to provide a recipe for a favorite family meal or to talk about what comfort food is for them. Once these are gathered, the class together can create recipe books with two or three favorite recipes from each family. These recipe books can then be shared with the rest of the families in the class, enabling families to learn more about the other kids in their children's class.

A third activity for incorporating difference in the classroom is to invite students to share pictures or stories about when a member of the family saw something that was not fair and what he or she did to try to make it right. This helps students ask questions at home with their parents that may bring up interesting situations of bias, perhaps that the child may or may not be aware of. In highlighting ways their parent tried to "make it right" or address the unfairness in some way, children are cultivating examples and role models not only from their own family but from others in the class about what standing up for others looks like.

3. Activity about Gender Norms: Who Gets to Make the Rules?

One way to discuss gender expectations (what is okay for "girls" but not "boys" or vice versa) is to invite children into a brainstorming session.[4] Ask them to come up with a list of things boys do or like and a list for what girls do or like. Then ask them, "Who made up these rules?" Children may come up with some interesting answers for who they think came up with the rules for what people of different genders can like or do.

Follow that question with others to see if there are any exceptions to these rules that they know of, either because they themselves like to do something on another gender's list or because they know someone who does. As a way to bridge the activity to other aspects of the child's life, invite them to find something that

---

[4]Adapted from Jennifer Bryan, *From the Dress-Up Corner to the Senior Prom: Navigating Gender and Sexuality Diversity in PreK–12 Schools* (Lanham, Md.: Rowman and Littlefield Education, 2012), xvi–xviii.

offers "proof" that there is an exception to a rule on the list. This may be a favorite sports jersey a girl likes to wear to show that girls can like sports too. Or a favorite doll that a boy likes to play with to show boys can play with dolls. The important thing is to help children think outside the box, to help them see how society makes up these rules, and to help them learn that they themselves can be part of changing those rules.

4. *Scripts for Parents: When Our Kids Say Embarrassing Things*

If you have had the experience of feeling embarrassed because your child has said something loudly in the supermarket about the appearance of a person close by, perhaps this section can help you reflect on that situation and prepare you for times when it may happen again. The kinds of comments young children make can be about a number of different things they notice about other people. Take the following examples, which will appear throughout the remaining sections of this appendix:

a.   "Why is that person sitting in that chair? What's wrong with them?"

b.   "That person looks like a man but I think it's a woman!"

c.   "Why is that man so dark?"

d.   "Those two women are holding hands!"

e.   "That woman is dressed so weird—why is her whole head covered?"

f.   "Why is that person sleeping outside on the sidewalk?"

First, Don't Panic

When your young child says something you feel is offensive, such as pointing to a grown-up or another child and remarking on their gender or race or calling attention to someone in a wheelchair and asking why they have to sit there, the first step is not to panic. The reason you should not panic is that you are not your best self when you panic; you may come across unkindly to your child, or you may even inadvertently communicate to your child that he or she is bad and should be ashamed of what they said. If this is what your child takes away from this interaction, they will be hesitant to make candid comments again.

Let's look first at your own response. How do you feel when your child says something inappropriate? Do you worry that their comments reflect poorly on you as a parent? It is important to remember that *your child is not a reflection of yourself.* Even if your child is not perfect in how they identify and talk about differences, you will be fine. No one will come at you and say "Aha! I knew it! Your child just showed me what a bigot you truly are!" The person about whom your child's comment was made may expect you to say something, but they still see you and your child as two separate people.

The common reaction many parents have is to feel embarrassed and to pretend that nothing happened. The child may notice that you are not responding, so it is possible that he or she may make the comment again to get your attention. If the first time embarrassed you, your child making the same comment twice will be even more embarrassing. If they are used to getting you to interact with them, and your reaction is like closing the door unexpectedly in their face, they will keep banging on the door until you acknowledge their presence. So in addition to not panicking, it is important to remember: *Do not ignore your child or their comment.*

Once you have taken a deep breath and you realize that your child is not a reflection of yourself, you choose not to ignore the child but to address the comment directly. Although your attention may have shifted to the person about whom the comment was made, worrying about their reaction and whether they heard your child's comment, make sure you turn your attention back to the child and be present to them.

Because of our tendency to be anxious in situations like this, a good acronym to help you remember a better response sounds like the sound you may be making in your head: "AAAA!" As in, "Agh! I'm not sure what to do!" Remembering the letter "A" as repeated in the sound "AAAA!" may help bring to mind other ways you can respond in the moment.

You have a few options: (1) *Affirm* your child's comment; (2) *Ask* questions to learn more about the child's thought process; (3) *Admit* what you don't know and answer with your best guess about the difference; and (4) *Allow* the other person to answer directly if they are willing to engage in a conversation.

The reason the first option is to *Affirm* the comment is because kids need to know that it is okay to notice difference. If we make them feel stupid or ashamed for asking their questions, they will stop asking them and will come to their own conclusions based on what they learn from society and what they pick up at school. Some of the conclusions they draw may not be as helpful as having a direct and honest discussion with you, their parent, in the moment. We also want children to grow up with a healthy and positive sense of who they are, and by affirming their comment or question, we are helping them build bridges across differences, encouraging them to keep asking and learning along the way.

1. Examples of *Affirming* your child's comment:

   a. "You're right, that person is in a special chair."

   b. "It sounds like you are noticing how that person looks like some people you know who are men, and they also look like people you know who are women."

   c. "Yes, you can see that he has a skin color that looks darker than your own."

   d. "Those two women *are* holding hands! You've got a good set of eyes."

   e. "That's a good question! I wonder why she is wearing that cover, too. I know some women dress that way because it is part of their religion."

   f. "You noticed that person sleeping there, and it surprised you since you sleep at home in a bed. Do you have any ideas about why he might be sleeping in that spot?"

Another option is to *Ask* questions about the child's comment or question, learning more about what made them notice that particular difference then. It may be that what felt embarrassing to you at first is actually an expression of care and concern, which should make a parent proud. If it embarrasses you to think that someone is assuming bad intentions of your child (mocking or pity), don't let others' assumptions lead you to jump to conclusions. Give your child the benefit of the doubt, trusting that there is a lot your child is trying to learn about the world, and discovering how to respond to differences is an important skill. Asking questions also allows you to probe for the deeper feelings at stake in these questions. Learning about differences can be scary when they make us question our own identities, so helping children face their fear of being wrong or needing to learn new things can help them accept their own feelings and move through any discomfort they may be feeling.

2. Examples of *Asking* questions about the comment:

    a. "When you noticed that man in the wheelchair, how did it make you feel? Have you ever seen anyone in a wheelchair before?

    b. "So far, you have been really good at putting things into categories. And the people you know are either boys or girls. How does it feel to see someone who is hard to put into a boy or girl category?

    c. "Who else do you know who has skin the same color as that man? Have you noticed differences in skin color among your friends?

    d. "Do you see other grown-ups holding hands sometimes? What does it mean to you to hold someone's hand? I wonder if they feel the way that you do when you hold hands?"

    e. "Do you have any guesses for why she may be wearing that? Do you ever wear anything special when we go to ____?" [Fill in the blank with what might be most understandable for your child: church, synagogue, grandparents' house, or another place where children may be expected to dress differently.]

f.   "How does it make you feel to see that man sleeping on the sidewalk?"

Once you've been able to learn a bit more about why your child made the comment or asked the question they did, you can follow up with your own best guess as to the answer to their question or thoughts about their comment. I say "best guess" because we need to let children know that whatever we say about this person is only a guess, unless we have actually gotten a chance to speak to him or her (which is the next option!). When we tell our children the reason why people are different in the way that they are, we may accidently slip into stereotyping. We may assume something about another person because we have knowledge about yet another person who shares that same difference in common, but their experiences may in fact be completely different. Let your child know that you are continuing to learn about other people, too, and that oftentimes the only way to know is to ask.

3. Examples of answering with your best guess and *Admitting* what you don't know:

a.   "Maybe he's in a wheelchair because he was born that way, or because he needs it to get around as fast as you and I."

b.   "Sometimes people don't feel like the categories of boy or girl really fit them. Maybe they were born with the body of a boy, but they feel inside like they are really a girl, or the other way around. And then some people just don't feel right with being a boy or a girl, and they feel like both."

c.   "There are a lot of different shades of skin color—some are lighter than others, some are darker than others, and even two babies born at the same time to the same mom can have different skin tones![5] I guess that's what makes people so beautiful—all the variety in the world."

d.　"I hold your hand because I'm your parent and I want to keep you close to me. Sometimes people hold hands because they really like each other, and it's a way of showing they like each other. Maybe you and a good friend at school like to hold hands sometimes. When people grow up, sometimes they hold hands with the person they love the most. Women can love women, men can love men, and women and men can love each other. My guess is that those two women love each other the best."

e.　"Some women dress that way to show a sign of respect to God, and also to keep people from being able to see their whole body. It might be because of their religion, or maybe just because they want to. I'm not sure."

f.　"I don't know why that man is sleeping on the ground. Some people sleep on the ground like that because they don't have a home. They're homeless. Sometimes that happens when people can't afford to live in their homes anymore. It makes me sad, but I know there are people in our city who are trying to help people who are homeless. Should we learn more about how people are trying to help?"

The fourth option in addressing your child's comment is to talk to the person who is the subject of your child's comment. This may feel the most awkward for you because this person may or may not be a stranger. How often do you come up to someone you don't know and begin a conversation that may or may not feel very sensitive? The opportunity here is to demonstrate to your child your own

---

[5]The *National Geographic Magazine* had on its cover in April 2018 twin daughters who look phenotypically different, with one girl having darker skin and dark hair, and the other having lighter skin and blonde hair. Showing these sisters may help convey the idea that there is only one human "race," and we come in all different shades and colors. To learn more, visit the National Geographic website: https://www.nationalgeographic.com/magazine/2018/04/race-issue-examination-understanding-background/.

capacity to keep learning about human difference, and for them to see you navigate conversations with someone who is different from yourself. As you show respect and courtesy to the person to whom your child has called attention, you can honor the attention your child has given to this particular person and ask if the other person is open to engaging your child. The key thing to remember here is not to assume the other person will say yes. If others are willing to share themselves with others, that is a gift, and if they choose not to, that is their right as well. We can demonstrate respect for others by asking the other person to engage, and if the answer is no, to say "thank you" and walk away, perhaps inviting your child to think of other ways the two of you can learn more together. Examples of ways you can approach the other person involved:

4. Examples of ways you can *Allow* the other person to answer directly:

    a. "Hello, excuse me. My name is ___, and my child was just wondering about your wheelchair. Would it be alright if he asked you some questions about it?" Then allow your child to direct the conversation, which may include questions like "How long have you had it?" and "Why do you need it?" If the person doesn't wish to answer any questions, simply say, "Of course. Thanks for your time, and sorry to bother you."

    b. "Hi. You may have overheard my child asking me a question about you. I was wondering if she could ask you about your gender? I told her not everyone identifies as a boy or a girl, and I was wondering if you would be willing to share with us your preferred pronouns?" Again, this may be something the person does not want to talk about, but if they are willing to help educate your child, you may hear them describing their own experience of gender in ways that help both you and your child understand better. If the person is not interested, again, a polite "Thank you, sorry to bother you" is appropriate.

c.   "Hello, how are you today? You may have overheard my child asking me about the color of your skin. I wanted him to know how people come in all different shades. Would it be ok if he compared his arm next to yours?" It may not be that you need to ask a question of the other person about their difference, but simply to acknowledge that they may have overheard you talking about them, in which case it would be polite to make contact and to help your child learn not to be shy around people from a different race or ethnic background.

d.   "Hi. My daughter noticed the two of you holding hands and she asked me about it. I told her that maybe you two really liked each other. Was that an accurate guess?" This may be a way to open the conversation in a friendly way, which could lead to more conversation or the opportunity for the couple to reply with a respectable "It's none of your business," to which you would respond: "Of course not. Thank you." Again, you never know if the people your child has commented about are in the mood or available to take time to educate you and your child, which is every bit their prerogative.

e.   "Excuse me. My child was asking me about the clothes you are wearing, and I guessed that maybe they were part of a religious belief or just because you want to wear them. Would you be so kind as to share with us more about your outfit?" If the person does not want to talk to you, they can always ignore you. If this happens, you can mention to your child that perhaps they were busy just then, and the two of you can learn more together at a later time. Again, the goal is to encourage curiosity as well as deep caring engagement, respecting that some people will want to talk with you, while others will not.[6]

---

[6]A great comic book written to answer some questions Muslim women get while wearing hijab is *Yes, I'm Hot in This: The Hilarious Truth of Life in a Hijab* by Huda Fahmy (Adams Media, 2018). Books can be a helpful and less intrusive way of getting to learn more about someone who is different from you.

f.   In the case of a person who is sleeping on the sidewalk, it is best not to wake them up. Personally, I do not like to be awakened from sleep, so I would not recommend doing this to a stranger. But if the person is awake, take stock of your own sense of their well-being. Do they seem to be making eye contact with others? If so, maybe they are open to conversation. If not, perhaps they would better like to be left alone. If your child is interested in learning more about homelessness, look into organizations in your community who may be offering respite for persons who are temporarily homeless. In such settings, persons may be willing to engage in conversation with others, and maybe you and your child together can learn more about their story. Either way, pay attention to your own feelings, and together with your child explore how learning about homelessness makes each of you feel.

In summary, children learn from an early age about some of the ways that people are different from one another. They notice gender and begin finding ways to categorize people based on what they perceive to be associated with being a boy or girl. They notice race and begin wondering about different skin colors and why people look the way they do. How parents and teachers handle children's questions and comments can inadvertently communicate that differences are bad and should be left alone. On the other hand, parents and teachers also have the opportunity to launch young children on a lifetime of working against bias in its many forms by seeing the gifts of diversity all around them.

II. Activities for Older Children and Youth

1. *Increasing Empathy with Youth: Living in the World HOUSE Activity*

Earlier in the book, we quoted Martin Luther King Jr., as saying that we are all living in a "world house" together. If we use the letters in the word "house" to form an acronym, it can be the basis for a learning activity with older children and youth. HOUSE: *Honor* that we come from different places; *Overcome* your initial stereotypes and biases about others; *Understand* that you're coming from a particular place too; *Share* your story; and *Empathize* with the other person. A shorthand way to remember this is to have youth say: "*Honor Others Understand Self: Empathy.*" Honoring others and understanding yourself is a way to have empathy for persons who are different from you. And talking about the metaphor of a world "house" where we are all together can emphasize the importance of empathy in a world of great diversity.

The metaphor of a world house can be helpful on another level: It reminds us of the houses in which we grew up. Within a single family, there can be a great number of differences. Children and youth already live with diversity in their own homes, and some of those differences may be harder to live with than others.

Think about your own upbringing. If you grew up with siblings, can you remember the kinds of fights you had with your brother or sister? If you have children of your own, how likely do you imagine it would be for them to want to live together in the future? My guess is that it would not be very likely, because knowing the ways that children behave with their siblings, it is unlikely that they will express a desire to share living space with one another indefinitely.

So why talk about a "world house" when we already know we do not want to live in close proximity to just anybody and everybody? When we may have already had bad experiences growing up with the people in our house, why turn to the image of a world house to talk about differences?

We can productively use the image of a world house for several reasons. The first is that as a metaphor it gives us the ability to gain some distance from the actual situations we are confronting. Talking about big issues that divide us can be tough, and talking in metaphor gives us a way of framing the conversation on a more neutral ground.

The second reason is that it conveys a sense of familiarity. Everyone grows up somewhere. Everyone comes from a place of some kind, and for that reason, it helps us to start with a similar frame of reference.

Third, having these kinds of conversations is risky, and talking about something as personal as our own homes is as if we are inviting one another into these intimate shared spaces. Talking about our differences in the context of the concrete experience of home life can help us not only get some distance via a metaphor, but get very close to one another in a shared sense of vulnerability.

Fourth, it provides a context for understanding the multiplicity of differences and commonalities we share and how those differences and similarities may be experienced even under one roof in our own homes. When we talk about differences, we are not talking simply about the "other"; we are also talking about ourselves with our spouses, kids, relatives, parents, siblings, and anyone we invite into our homes. In each of these relationships, we come across opportunities to engage in conversations about difference. We learn the language of difference in our own homes.

THE WORLD HOUSE ACTIVITY: TALKING ABOUT HOME THROUGH THE SENSES

When talking with older children, it is helpful to be specific about the ways in which children are different from and similar to each other. You can use this exercise to engage children in elementary school and older to connect things they are already learning in school to the ways they come from different homes.

Start by asking children to think about their homes. Where do they live? How do they get there? When they come home from school, what does coming "home" look like to them? Do they walk upstairs into an apartment? Or do they walk to the front door of a house? Are they dropped off by a bus and then walk to where they live? Or do they arrive home with a parent or caregiver?

Asking children to describe what they do at the end of the school day can help to name some of the ways that they are different, and how they are similar. For instance, all of them have a "home." It may be a home they have known for a long time, or a home that is new to them. For students who have moved recently from somewhere else, they may have more than one image of what is home to them. How many homes have children known in their lifetimes?

Continuing to share about the home, children can describe who makes up the other people in their home. Do they live with parents? Do they have siblings? Do they have parents who live in two different homes that they alternate visiting? Are their parents the same gender? Do they live with one parent? Are there additional caregivers in the home? Maybe they live with a grandparent or an aunt as well. If all of the people with whom they live were in a single room, how crowded would the room be?

Children can explore this image of their family through the senses: What do the people they live with *look* like? Do they all look similar to one another, or do they all look different? Maybe one parent has dark skin and another lighter skin. Maybe one parent uses a wheelchair. Maybe one parent wears a beautiful sari around the house.

What do the people they live with *sound* like? Does everyone speak the same language, or are other languages spoken at home? Are some family members loud, and others quiet? What kind of music do members of their family listen to?

Can they identify a certain *smell* with members of their family? For example, maybe a grandparent they live with smells like peppermint, or their father who cooks a lot smells like certain spices, or their brother who works in a restaurant smells like pizza.

The composition of a family can change over time, and outside stresses can affect the composition of a family. Worries about deportation and citizenship status, working late shifts or constant travel that may prevent a family member from being present with the child, changes in the health of a caregiver, the birth or adoption of another sibling—all can shift a child's family.

Inviting children to share these differences can help them to see how much they have in common with others, as well as to understand that their differences can make their classroom more interesting. The ways we are different from one another provide opportunity for us to learn new things, to see the world from a different perspective, and to grow in our understanding of what it means to be human. Giving children an opportunity to share these differences and similarities with others can help them deepen their capacity to be inclusive and accepting of others' difference.

As a teacher or parent, it is important that you consider the ways that your own upbringing was different from and similar to that of the children in your life. As children go through this exercise, you can share your own examples.

FOR TEENAGERS

In working with youth as parents or teachers, using the senses may seem too elementary for them. Instead, you could have them take it to the next level. Perhaps you can use this exercise to start a writing project—poetry or autobiography—and let youth use their creativity to consider the uniqueness of where they come from.

This can also be a jumping-off point for imagining the experiences of persons who are different from them. Invite youth to consider themselves as a guest in someone else's home, particularly someone they do not get along with or who comes from a different background. Have them picture themselves walking into the house. You can follow a script:

"You've come to the door of a person you may not know well. Perhaps this is someone you haven't gotten along with in the past, but for some reason, they have kindly invited you over to their home. What did you notice as you walked up to their home? Maybe there are flowers in a pot that need to be watered. Or maybe there are bottles of sunscreen and bug spray sitting outside the door. Or maybe the family's shoes are all laid out neatly in rows.

"You knock on the door. When they open the door and invite you in, you walk into a hallway or a family room, a large space you enter just as you come through the door. There might be a couch, a chair, a rug. Maybe it feels really informal and cozy. Or maybe it feels formal, like only for grown-ups. Imagine this space as you walk in and look around. What do you see?

"As you imagine the family room of this other person, think about the family into which you were born or adopted. As you emerged into this world, what were the sights and sounds that greeted you? What was *family* for you?"

We bring all of our family memories into the family room of the world house. We experience other people's families, and we compare them to our own. We may find a great many similarities, and we may encounter great differences. But we first come into the world through our family, and it is these people and our relationships with them that form our understanding of human difference.

What we know from our family, this is *familiar*. The people we meet outside of our family are new to us at first, and maybe we sense stranger danger, a fear of the unknown, an awareness of difference in them. At an early age, we distinguish between what is familiar and what is different by what we experience in our own family. Before we are conscious of thought, we learn to recognize faces and smile in response to the ones we know.

Picture your own family room, and imagine it filled with familiar things. What are the things that hang on the wall? What does your furniture look like? What pictures do you see in frames? What colors do you see? What can you smell? What kind of texture do you notice?

Now, in this family room, you are not alone. Imagine the person who invited you into their home is there with you in yours. Imagine your two family rooms linked together. You can easily step from your family room into theirs just by walking through a doorway. Now picture that there are more than these two family rooms—you cannot see them all, but there are people in family rooms of their own, lined up next to yours for infinity. On and on, room after room, each person has entered their home, and they are noticing the sights and sounds and smells of the room of their family.

Imagine a doorway connecting all of these family rooms. Go through the room of the person who invited you into their home to the far end, where there is another door. You knock and find that someone else opens the door for you and welcomes you in. You are now crossing over into their family room.

This is a person who looks very much like you, but you do not know them very well. Who is it? A classmate? Someone you have seen in a movie or on a TV show? The family room you enter with them is entirely new to you. New sights, new sounds, new smells. The furniture is different, the color schemes and textures are different from your own. This person who looks so much like you has such a different family room from your own. Who do you see in the pictures they have in frames?

We do not know how much our own family has shaped us until we spend time with someone else in their own home with their family. Did you find yourself comparing the two experiences and judging one way of doing things as better than the other?

Returning to the HOUSE acronym, remember that the goal of talking about our homes and where we come from is to Honor Others, Understand Self, and Empathize. As we walk into another person's home, we are being treated with hospitality, and we need to honor our host. As we think about our own homes and realize that we come from specific places, we begin to understand ourselves better and see how our own family has shaped what we think and how we view the world. By doing this exercise of honoring others and understanding ourselves, we are learning to Empathize. We are trying to honor the similarities between us and respect our differences.

2. The ROCKS of our Foundation

As children and youth share their own experiences and differences with one another, it is important to establish guidelines for how they should treat one another in the midst of that vulnerable space. One way to do this is to talk about the importance of having a good foundation. Using the acronym ROCKS can help remind young people of the attitudes that will make these conversations and times of sharing feel more hospitable to one another.

Respect, Optimism, Community, Kindness, Safety: using the first letter from each of these words forms the acronym ROCKS, which represents the foundation for how we can engage our differences. These values—respect, optimism, community, kindness, and safety—can help us see one another as an integral part of our shared effort to build a peaceful and just world.

Respect is foundational, because no matter what our differences, each and every person is worthy of being treated with dignity.

Optimism is an important component because entering these conversations with hope that things *can* get better keeps us open to ideas that the "other side" might be offering to us.

Community is a central value of this process, because we are all living in a world house and we need to make decisions based on how we can best grow in community with one another.

Kindness is a crucial support to this work because however we have come to this moment in time, we all carry our own wounds and struggles, and treating one another with kindness is how we ourselves want and need to be treated.

Safety finishes off this fivefold set of foundational values; because even with our best efforts and optimistic hopes for the future, we are aware that some in our society are more vulnerable than others, that whole groups have been victims of hate crimes and discrimination, and we need to keep their need for safety in the forefront of our conversations. As we look at the result of our work together, can we say with confidence that this will help those communities in fact be *more* safe? Or will the results of our deliberations actually lead to *less* safety for those who are already vulnerable?

Let these ROCKS form a foundation in your own work of helping people in your community learn the ABCs of diversity, and may you find courage to continue the life-sustaining work of creating the world house.

3. *Relearning Our History: Challenging Traditional Curriculum Lessons*

Another significant curricular activity for older children and teenagers is to look at the varieties of ways in which we learn about history. For instance, even though children notice race from an early age, racism is often not discussed in the official school curriculum. For parents, it is important that you track what your child is learning in school and help supplement the stories they are learning from the main curriculum with stories of people who may tell the story from a different point of view. It may be that the curriculum tells only part of the story, particularly the part of the story as it is told by white people. You can help youth understand the world in which we live by giving them a broader base of knowledge besides what is included in the history textbooks. For instance, you can introduce youth to stories and biographies featuring a main character of a different race or ethnicity from your child or the majority of students in your class.

I (Carolyn) have tried to do this with my own children regarding Texas history. Just as when I was growing up, children in grades four and seven going through Texas public schools take a year of Texas history. In fifth grade, students learn about slavery and the Civil War, but they do not typically learn much about slavery in Texas (if they focus on it at all). Leaving out this information communicates to children that slavery only took place in other parts in the South, but not in Texas. It was not until I was thirty-five, having returned to live in Texas after being away for my career and education, that I discovered Randolph Campbell's book *An Empire for Slavery: Texas and the Peculiar Institution*, in which Campbell describes how the founding father of Texas, Stephen F. Austin, not only had slaves, but sought independence from Mexico because the new Mexican government outlawed slavery.[7] Why did I not learn about this when learning about Texas history in grade school? As someone with a strong Texan identity, it was important for me to question the assumptions built into my education of Texas history, seeing white people as "Texans" more readily than someone who is African American or Hispanic, even though there have been indigenous, Latino/a, and African American Texans living in this region long before "Texas" was a state. And growing up seeing Mexico as the "enemy" that Texans fought to win their independence, it was a flip of the script to realize that Mexico had abolished slavery, while white Texans were trying to hold on to their freedom to withhold freedom from blacks.

---

[7]Randolph Campbell, *An Empire for Slavery: Texas and the Peculiar Institution 1821–1865* (Baton Rouge: Louisiana State University Press, 1989).

Our Founding Myths Shattered and Remade as Black: The 1619 Project[8]

Recently, I discovered that it was not just my Texas origin myth that needed rethinking. The story of America's "birth" also needed to be retold. Here is a quotation from a *New York Times Magazine* special issue called "The 1619 Project": "Conveniently left out of our founding mythology is the fact that one of the primary reasons the colonists decided to declare their independence from Britain was because they wanted to protect the institution of slavery."[9] Just as Texas's independence was closely linked to the preservation of slavery in Texas, so too was the fight for American independence from Britain. But that is not the only challenge to our origin myth of the founding of America.

Reading through the entire special issue "The 1619 Project," you get the sense that the way we tell American history will never be the same. The authors, under the leadership of Nikole Hannah-Jones, put together essay after essay unpacking the significance of slavery to so many of the quintessentially "American" institutions that make up the United States. Marking the four hundredth anniversary of the first black people in America, this issue takes back the narrative of the "Negro problem" and instead sees in black people the meaning of what makes an American. Some of the articles are gruesome but not unexpected, such as Linda Villarosa's essay on the cruel torture inflicted upon African American bodies as a way to experiment with medicine and study the differences between blacks and whites.[10] Others run to the very core of our national myth of origin, as a country for the people and by the people, such as the essay on democracy written by Jamelle Bouie.[11] Even the mundane experiences of life in the United States—such as traffic—are revealed as originating in race-based animosity and segregation.[12] The issue

---

[8]*The New York Times Magazine,* August 18, 2019 issue, special edition "The 1619 Project." The entire issue is available online with suggested resources for using the material in educational contexts: https://www.nytimes.com/interactive/2019/08/14/magazine/1619-america-slavery.html.

[9]Nikole Hannah-Jones "The Idea of America," in "The 1619 Project," 18.

[10]Linda Villarosa, "Medical Inequality," in "The 1619 Project," 57.

[11]Jamelle Bouie, "Undemocratic Democracy," in "The 1619 Project," 50.

[12]Kevin M. Kruse, "Traffic," in "The 1619 Project," 48.

looks at the way slavery affected the global market economy, with enslavers using their enslaved "property" to gain mortgages to pay for farm equipment and more land; such mortgages were bundled together by state banks and sold as "bonds," the beginning of our bond system of trading.[13] Even the very name of "Wall Street" itself stems from an actual wall built by enslaved people, which served as a public auction for the buying and selling of black women and men.[14] The essays, individually and collectively, offer a narrative of the United States that sees as its origin not the year 1776 with the Declaration of Independence, but the year 1619, when twenty to thirty enslaved people arrived on a boat and were sold to the Jamestown colonists.

This is an origin story that shifts the narrative entirely. It takes the central stage away from white "founding fathers" and gives it to the black women and men who survived the Middle Passage, who created their own culture and religion when stripped of the cultures and religions of their ancestral homes, who learned to read and write even though it was against the law, and who even died fighting in our wars for a country that regularly denied them the rights of full citizens.[15]

I read "The 1619 Project" from cover to cover the week it came out, and I felt the world shift under my feet. I could no longer think about the sugar in all of our foods or the cotton in my clothes without thinking about the black men and women who died in forced labor camps known as plantations to grow these agricultural crops.

As a woman, I could not consider the fight for equal rights and pay without remembering the efforts of black men newly elected to congress in the years of Reconstruction right after the Civil War, who led the way for all other marginalized groups fighting for equal rights. The passage of the 13th, 14th, and 15th Amendments to the

---

[13]Matthew Desmond, "Capitalism," in "The 1619 Project," 30.

[14]Tiya Miles, "Municipal Bonds: How Slavery Built Wall Street," in "The 1619 Project," 40.

[15]See Hannah-Jones, "The Idea of America, p. 14; and Yusef Komunyakaa on Crispus Attucks, "The First American to Die for the Cause of Independence," in "The 1619 Project," 29.

Constitution happened in those early years of Reconstruction, after the assassination of President Lincoln but before removal of federal troops from the South and the reign of White terror that stripped from many blacks in the South their newly won rights.[16]

As someone who enjoys good healthcare, I can no longer take for granted my own access to quality healthcare as a white person in a system designed for white people. In her article on our healthcare system, Jeneen Interlandi argues that any success our nation has had in making healthcare available to all, including Medicare, Medicaid, and the Affordable Health Care Act, has happened only because of the insistence of the National Medical Association—the leading black medical organization—that had long been excluded from the American Medical Association.[17] It was the NMA that first argued that healthcare was a basic human right, particularly during the 1960s when Medicare and Medicaid were being established, while at the same time the AMA was saying that giving healthcare to all was socialist and anti-American. The insistence against healthcare for all came largely from Southern Democrats, who also made it harder for black workers to have other benefits that would contribute to greater overall wellbeing and health, such as safer working conditions and Social Security. Nearly half of all black people in the nation at the time worked in agriculture and domestic labor, two industries explicitly excluded from benefits given through the New Deal legislation that required a minimum wage, fair working conditions including the eight-hour work day, and the right for workers to unionize. So at the same time that white workers were able to unionize and get fairer wages and begin accruing the benefits of Social Security, most blacks were prevented from getting jobs in any of the industries that provided these benefits. Blacks were forced to work in conditions that exceeded the federal mandates, were paid less for their efforts, and were unable to take advantage of social safety nets that supported people when they became sick or disabled. The ongoing disparity in health outcomes between whites and blacks should not surprise us. Interlandi quotes

---

[16]Hannah-Jones, "The Idea of America," 21.
[17]Jeneen Interlandi, "A Broken Healthcare System," in "The 1619 Project," 45.

Harvard historian Evelynn Hammonds: "There has never been any period in American history where the health of blacks was equal to that of whites. Disparity is built into the system."[18]

In another essay, Linda Villarosa discloses why such disparity still exists: ongoing belief in the medical myths that were created to justify slavery, arguing that black people were physiologically different than white people.[19] Villarosa describes the horrific torture inflicted upon John Brown by Dr. Thomas Hamilton in the 1820s and 1830s in order for Dr. Hamilton to "prove" his theory that black skin was thicker than white skin. Another doctor, J. Marion Sims, known as the "father of gynecology," believed another frequently touted belief to justify the harsh conditions of slavery: that blacks had a higher pain threshold than whites. With this in mind, Sims subjected black women to unimaginable pain by cutting on their genitals to practice surgical techniques. The pain was unimaginable to Sims, because he believed they felt less pain than he did. Villarosa's essay also points to a 2016 survey of 222 white medical students, in which more than half of the respondents believed at least one of these myths. Believing that someone has thicker skin or experiences less pain in turn makes doctors less likely to prescribe proper treatment for illness. The history of the treatment of black Americans by our healthcare system makes their ongoing survival and health a miracle of black perseverance.

When we think about who counts as "American," these essays point us to an archetype of resistance, grit, and ingenuity: blacks. To be black is to be truly American. As Nikole Hannah-Jones writes in her introductory essay, "What if America understood, finally, in this 400th year, that we have never been the problem, but the solution?"[20]

Part of our education as adults, as well as parents, requires learning how persons in our society have been marginalized in the past and yet have overcome great adversity in order to thrive, and that *this* is what it means to be American, that this is the American

[18]Interlandi, "A Broken Healthcare System," 45.
[19]Villarosa, "Medical Inequality," 57.
[20]Hannah-Jones, "The Idea of America," 26.

dream. While for many, living in this country has been a nightmare rather than a dream, they are living lives of courage and resistance and hope, pointing all of us to a better dream than the one we could have imagined on our own.

Activity: With teenagers, share Carolyn's description of her own discovery of the role of slavery in Texas history and her comments and reflections on the 1619 Project. Have students pick an article from the 1619 Project (available online) to read and reflect on. Afterwards, invite students to share in what ways this project has helped them relearn history.

For other curriculum discussions and lesson plans, see the Pulitzer Center's website dedicated to the 1619 Project: https://pulitzercenter.org/lesson-plan-grouping/1619-project-curriculum.

For more curriculum ideas, go to our website at www.abcsofdiversity.com, and find out how others are building community by helping one another to embrace our differences.

Bibliography

1001 Inventions & Awesome Facts from Muslim Civilization.
Washington, D.C.: National Geographic, 2012.

Achtemeier, Mark. *The Bible's YES to Same-Sex Marriage: An Evangelical's Change of Heart.* Louisville: Westminster John Knox Press, 2014.

Alcantara, Jared. *Crossover Preaching: Intercultural-Improvisational Homiletics in Conversation with Gardner C. Taylor.* Downers Grove, IL: InterVarsity Press, 2015.

Alexander, Kwame. *The Crossover.* Boston, MA: Houghton Mifflin Harcourt, 2019.

———. *Rebound.* Boston, MA: Houghton Mifflin Harcourt, 2018.

Anderson, Ashaunta, MD, MPH, MSHS, FAAP, and Jacqueline Dougé, MD, MPH, FAAP. "Talking to Children About Racial Bias." Healthychildren.org. American Academy of Pediatrics, 2019. https://www.healthychildren.org/English/healthy-living/emotional-wellness/Building-Resilience/Pages/Talking-to-Children-About-Racial-Bias.aspx.

Anderson, Carol. *White Rage: the Unspoken Truth of Our Racial Divide.* New York: Bloomsbury, 2017.

Andrews, Arin. *Some Assembly Required: the Not-so-Secret Life of a Transgender Teen.* Toronto: CNIB, 2016.

Ang, Soon, and Linn Van Dyne, "Conceptualization of Cultural Intelligence," in *Handbook of Cultural Intelligence: Theory, Measurement, and Applications.* Armonk, NY: M.E. Sharpe, 2008.

Appiah, Kwame Anthony. *The Lies That Bind: Rethinking Identity.* New York: Liveright Publishing, 2018.

Asani, Ali. "On Pluralism, Intolerance, and the Qur'an." The Institute of Ismaili Studies. Accessed Dec. 24, 2019. https://iis.ac.uk/pluralism-intolerance-and-qur.

Bailey, Eric. *The New Face of America: How the Emerging Multiracial, Multiethnic Majority Is Changing the United States.* Santa Barbara, CA: Praeger, 2013.

Beirich, Heidi. "Trump's Anti-Muslim Words and Policies Have Consequences," Southern Poverty Law Center. April 24, 2018. https://www.splcenter.org/news/2018/04/24/trumps-anti-muslim-words-and-policies-have-consequences.

Bell, Cece. *El Deafo*. New York: Amulet Books, 2014.

Berger, Michele W. "Social Media Use Increases Depression and Loneliness." *Penn Today*. November 9, 2018. https://penntoday.upenn.edu/news/social-media-use-increases-depression-and-loneliness.

Bigelow, Lisa Jenn. *Drum Roll, Please*. New York: Harper, 2018.

Birdwhistell, Ray. *Introduction to Kinesics: An Annotation System for Analysis of Body Motion and Gesture*. Louisville: University of Louisville, 1979.

Bouie, Jamelle. "Undemocratic Democracy," in "The 1619 Project." *The New York Times*, August 14, 2019.

Brill, Stephanie A., and Rachel Pepper. *The Transgender Child: A Handbook for Families and Professionals*. New Westminster, B.C.: Post Hypnotic Press, 2011.

Bryan, Jennifer. *From the Dress-Up Corner to the Senior Prom: Navigating Gender and Sexuality Diversity in Pre K–12 Schools*. Lanham, MD: Rowman and Littlefield Education, 2012.

Callahan, Gerald. *Between XX and XY: Intersexuality and the Myth of Two Sexes*. Chicago, IL: Chicago Review Press, 2009.

Campbell, Randolph. *An Empire for Slavery: Texas and the Peculiar Institution 1821–1865*. Baton Rouge, LA: Louisiana State University Press, 1989.

Cartaya, Pablo. *The Epic Fail of Arturo Zamora*. New York: Puffin Books, 2017.

Chanani, Nidhi. *Pashmina*. New York: First Second, 2017.

Choi, Yangsook. *The Name Jar*. Decorah, IA: Dragonfly Books, 2003.

Cline-Ransome, Lesa. *Game Changers: the Story of Venus and Serena Williams*. Simon & Schuster/Paula Wiseman Books, 2018.

Combs, Bobbie. *ABC a Family Alphabet Book*. Annapolis, MD: Two Lives Publishing, 2012.

Curtis, Christopher Paul. *Bud, Not Buddy.* Lawrence, MA: Small
	Planet Communications, 2002.

Dee, Barbara. *Star Crossed.* New York. Aladdin, 2017.

Deluca, Stephanie, Susan Clampet-Lundquist, and Kathryn Edin.
	Coming of Age in the Other America. New York: Russell Sage
	Foundation, 2016.

"Demographics of Social Media Users and Adoption in the United
	States." Pew Research Center: Internet, Science & Tech.
	Accessed December 27, 2019. https://www.pewinternet.
	org/fact-sheet/social-media/.

Derman-Sparks, Louise, and Julie Olsen Edwards. *Anti-Bias
	Education for Young Children and Ourselves.* Washington,
	D.C.: National Association of Education of Young
	Children.

Desmond, Matthew. "Capitalism," in "The 1619 Project." *The New
	York Times*, August 14, 2019.

DiOrio, Rana, Emma D. Dryden, and Ken Min. *What Does It Mean
	to Be an Entrepreneur?* New York: Scholastic, 2016.

Draper, Sharon M. *Blended.* New York: Atheneum Books for Young
	Readers, 2018.

———. *Out of My Mind.* New York: Atheneum Books for Young
	Readers, 2012.

Eberhardt, Jennifer. *Biased: Uncovering the Hidden Prejudice that
	Shapes What We See, Think, and Do.* New York: Viking,
	2019.

Edwards, Sue Bradford, and Duchess Harris. *Black Lives Matter.*
	Minneapolis: Essential Library, 2016.

EmbraceRace. "31 Children's Books to Support Conversations on
	Race, Racism and Resistance." Embracerace.org. Accessed
	December 30, 2019. https://www.embracerace.org/blog/26-
	childrens-books-to-support-conversations-on-race-racism-
	resistance.

Fahmy, Huda. *Yes, I'm Hot in This: The Hilarious Truth of Life in a
	Hijab.* Avon, MA: Adams Media, 2018.

Fox, Mem, and Leslie Staub. *Whoever You Are.* Boston, MA:
	Houghton Mifflin Harcourt, 2017.

Frey, William. *Diversity Explosion.* Washington, D.C.: The
          Brookings Institution, 2018.
Gibson, Carrie. *El Norte: The Epic and Forgotten Story of Hispanic
          North America.* New York: Atlantic Monthly Press, 2019.
Gillman, Melanie. *As the Crow Flies.* Chicago, IL: Iron Circus
          Comics, 2018.
Gino, Alex. *George.* New York: Scholastic Inc., 2018.
Goldberg, Lesley. "Why 'Grey's Anatomy' Just Overtly Tackled
          Unconscious Bias," *The Hollywood Reporter,* January 25,
          2018, https://www.hollywoodreporter.com/live-feed/
          why-greys-anatomy-just-overtly-tackled-unconscious-
          bias-1078509.
Grey's Anatomy, season 14, episode 10. "Personal Jesus." Directed
          by Kevin Rodney Sullivan, written by Zoanne Clack. Aired
          January 25, 2018 on ABC.
Hale, Nathan. *The Underground Abductor.* New York: Scholastic,
          2017.
Hall, Michael. *Red: A Crayon's Story.* New York: Greenwillow Books,
          2015.
Hannah-Jones, Nikole. "The Idea of America," in "The 1619
          Project." *The New York Times*, August 14, 2019.
Harney, John. "How Do Sunni and Shia Islam Differ?" *The
          New York Times,* Jan. 3, 2016. https://www.nytimes.
          com/2016/01/04/world/middleeast/q-and-a-how-do-sunni-
          and-shia-islam-differ.html.
Harvard Divinity School. "Religion and the Feminist Movement
          Conference - Panel IV: Delores S. Williams." Filmed
          November, 2002. Youtube video, 17:00. Posted June 2014.
          https://www.youtube.com/watch?v=hltJgzbXPFI.
Harvey, Jennifer, and Tim J. Wise. *Raising White Kids: Bringing up
          Children in a Racially Unjust America.* Nashville: Abingdon
          Press, 2018.
Haynes, Trevor. "Dopamine, Smartphones & You: A
          Battle for Your Time." *Science in the News,* May 1,
          2018. http://sitn.hms.harvard.edu/flash/2018/
          dopamine-smartphones-battle-time/.

Helms, Janet E. *Black and White Racial Identity: Theory, Research, and Practice.* Westport, CT: Praeger Publishers, 1990.

Henry, William III. "Beyond the Melting Pot." *Time*, April 9, 1990.

Herthel, Jessica, Jazz Jennings, and Shelagh McNicholas. *I Am Jazz!* New York: Dial Books for Young Readers, 2014.

Hill, Katie Rain. *Rethinking Normal: a Memoir in Transition.* Toronto: CNIB, 2016.

Hira, Nadira. "Why the Fight Against Racism Has to Start with Owning It." *Newsweek*, August 22, 2019. https://www.newsweek.com/2019/08/30/fight-against-racism-owning-it-1455229.html.

"His Highness the Aga Khan." *The Ismaili.* Accessed Dec. 24, 2019. https://the.ismaili/his-highness-aga-khan.

Home, directed by Tim Johnson. USA: DreamWorks Animation, 2015.

Horton, Daryl, and Neil Blumofe. "Commentary: Why We, a Reverend and a Rabbi, Travel to Witness America." *Austin American-Statesman,* September 10, 2019. https://www.statesman.com/opinion/20190910/commentary-why-we-reverend-and-rabbi-travel-to-witness-america

Interlandi, Jeneen. "A Broken Healthcare System," in "The 1619 Project." *The New York Times*, 2019.

James, Kelly Clark et al. *101 Key Terms in Philosophy and Their Importance for Theology.* Louisville: Westminster John Knox Press, 2004.

Jennings, Jazz. *Being Jazz: My Life as a (Transgender) Teen.* New York: Ember, 2017.

Johnson, Dolores, and Virginia Schomp. *The Harlem Renaissance.* Tarrytown, NY: Marshall Cavendish Benchmark, 2008.

Jones, Charisse, and Kumea Shorter-Gooden. *Shifting: The Double Lives of Black Women in America.* New York: HarperCollins, 2003.

Jones, Phyllis, Benedict I. Truman, and Laurie D. Elam-Evans, et al. "Using 'Socially Assigned Race' to Probe White Advantages in Health Status." *Ethnicity & Disease* 18, no. 4 (Autumn 2008).

Kadohata, Cynthia. *Kira-Kira*. New York: Atheneum Books for Young Readers, 2005.

Kasasa. "Boomers, Gen X, Gen Y, and Gen Z Explained." *Kasasa.com*, https://www.kasasa.com/articles/generations/gen-x-gen-y-gen-z.

Katz, Karen. *The Colors of Us*. New York: Henry Holt, 1999.

Kendi, Ibram X. *How to Be an Antiracist*. London: The Bodley Head, 2019.

Khan, Hena. *Amina's Voice*. Waterville, ME: Thorndike Press, 2019.

Khan, Hena, and Aaliya Jaleel. *Under My Hijab*. New York: Lee & Low Books, 2019.

Khan, Hena, and Mehrdokht Amini. *Golden Domes and Silver Lanterns: A Muslim Book of Colors*. San Francisco, CA: Chronicle Books, 2015.

King, Martin Luther, Jr., *Where Do We Go from Here: Chaos or Community?* Boston, MA: Beacon Press, 2010.

Klass, Perri. "The Impact of Racism on Children's Health," *The New York Times,* August 12, 2019. https://www.nytimes.com/2019/08/12/well/family/the-impact-of-racism-on-childrens-health.html.

Komunyakaa, Yusef. "The First American to Die for the Cause of Independence," in "The 1619 Project." *The New York Times*, August 14, 2019.

Kruse, Kevin M. "Traffic," in "The 1619 Project." *The New York Times*, August 14, 2019.

Kuklin, Susan. *Beyond Magenta: Transgender Teens Speak Out*. Somerville, MA: Candlewick Press, 2014.

LeVay, Simon. *Gay, Straight, and the Reason Why: The Science of Sexual Orientation,* 2d ed. New York: Oxford University Press, 2017.

Livermore, David. *Cultural Intelligence: Improving Your CQ to Engage Our Multicultural World*. Grand Rapids, MI: Baker Academic, 2009.

Love, Jessica. *Julian Is a Mermaid*. London: Walker Books, 2019.

Lowry, Lois. *Number the Stars*. New York: Houghton Mifflin Books for Children, 1989.

Masci, David, Anna Brown, and Jocelyn Kiley. "5 Facts about Same-Sex Marriage." Pew Research Center, June 24, 2019. https://www.pewresearch.org/fact-tank/2019/06/24/same-sex-marriage.

McClaurin, Irma, and Virginia Schomp. *The Civil Rights Movement.* Tarrytown, NY: Marshall Cavendish Benchmark, 2008.

Miles, Tiya. "Municipal Bonds: How Slavery Built Wall Street," in "The 1619 Project." *The New York Times*, August 14, 2019.

Ministry of Social Justice and Empowerment, Government of India. *Report of the Expert Committee on the Issues Relating to Transgender Persons*. Expert Committee on the Issues Relating to Transgender Persons. New Delhi, India, 2017. http://socialjustice.nic.in/writereaddata/UploadFile/Binder2.pdf.

Mixed-Ish, season 1, episode 3. "Let Your Hair Down." Directed by Michael Spiller, written by Karin Gist and Peter Saji. Aired October 8, 2019, on ABC.

"Mother's Worksheet for Child's Birth Certificate." Centers for Disease Control and Prevention. Accessed December 23, 2019. https://www.cdc.gov/nchs/data/dvs/moms-worksheet-2016-508.pdf

Mottahedeh, Roy. "Towards an Islamic Theology of Toleration," in *Islamic Law Reform and Human Rights*. Nordic Human Rights Publications, 1992.

Mukhi, Misbah, and Areebah Ajani. "Texas Governor and Community Officials Inaugurate New Ismaili Jamatkhana," *the.Ismaili,* August 22, 2018. https://the.ismaili/usa/texas-governor-and-community-officials-inaugurate-new-jamatkhana

Nazario, Tiarra. *And That's Why She's My Mama*. United States: Tiarra Nazario, 2018

Newman Lesléa, and Carol Thompson. Mommy, Mama, and Me. Berkeley, CA: Tricycle Press, 2009.

Noble, Safiya. *Algorithms of Oppression*. New York: New York University Press, 2018.

Ortiz, Paul. *An African American and Latinx History of the United States*. Boston, MA: Beacon Press, 2018.

Ortiz, Vilma, and Edward Telles. "Racial Identity and Racial Treatment of Mexican Americans," *Race and Social Problems* 4, no. 1 (April 2012), https://www.ncbi.nlm.nih.gov/pmc/articles/PMC3846170/.

Owens-Reid, Dannielle, and Kristin Russo. *This Is a Book for Parents of Gay Kids: a Question & Answer Guide to Everyday Life*. San Francisco, CA: Chronicle Books, 2014.

O'Neill, Katie. *Princess Princess Ever After*. Portland, OR: Oni Press, 2016.

Park, Linda Sue. *A Long Walk to Water: Based on a True Story*. London: Rock the Boat, 2018.

Parr, Todd. *We Belong Together: A Book About Adoption and Families*. Sydney, N.S.W.: ABC Books for the Australian Broadcasting Corporation, 2008.

Pearlman, Robb, and Eda Kaban. *Pink Is for Boys*. New York: Running Press Kids, 2018.

Penfold, Alexandra, and Suzanne Kaufman. *All Are Welcome*. London: Bloomsbury Children's Books, 2019.

Pollack, David C., Ruth E. Van Reken, and Michael V. Pollack. *Third Culture Kids 3rd Edition: Growing Up Among Worlds*. Boston, MA: Nicholas Brealey, 2017.

Project Implicit. Accessed December 23, 2019. https://implicit.harvard.edu/implicit

Pulitzer Center. "The 1619 Project Curriculum." Pulitzercenter.org. Accessed December 30, 2019. https://pulitzercenter.org/lesson-plan-grouping/1619-project-curriculum.

Rabin, Roni Caryn. "Huge Racial Disparities Found in Deaths Linked to Pregnancy." *The New York Times*, May 7, 2019. https://www.nytimes.com/2019/05/07/health/pregnancy-deaths-.html?searchResultPosition=1&module=inline.

Rhodes, Jewell Parker. *Ghost Boys*. New York: Little, Brown and Company, 2019.

Richardson, Justin, Peter Parnell, and Henry Cole. *And Tango Makes Three*. New York: Little Simon, 2015.

Roediger, David. *Working Toward Whiteness: How America's Immigrants Became White*. New York: Basic Book, 2005.

Rogers, Katie, and Nicholas Fandos. "Trump Tells Congresswomen to 'Go Back' to the Countries They Came From." *The New York Times,* July 14, 2019. https://www.nytimes.com/2019/07/14/us/politics/trump-twitter-squad-congress.html.

Rubin, Adam, and Crash McCreery. *El Chupacabras*. New York: The Dial Press, 2018.

Ryan, Pam Muñoz. *Echo: a Novel*. New York: Scholastic Inc., 2016.

———. *Esperanza Rising*. Waterville, ME: Thorndike Press, 2018.

Ryle, Robyn. *She, He, They, Me: for the Sisters, Misters, and Binary Resisters*. Naperville, IL: Sourcebooks, Inc., 2019.

Sachedina, Abdulaziz. *The Islamic Roots of Democratic Pluralism*. New York: Oxford University Press, 2001.

Sanders, Cody. *A Brief Guide to Ministry with LGBTQIA Youth*. Louisville: Westminster John Knox Press, 2017.

Sanders, Rob, and Jamey Christoph. *Stonewall: A Building. an Uprising. a Revolution*. New York: Random House, 2019.

"School Climate Survey." GLSEN. Accessed December 23, 2019. https://www.glsen.org/research/school-climate-survey.

Senker, Cath. *Taking Action against Racism*. New York: Rosen Central, 2010.

Silva, Kumarini. *Brown Threat: Identification in the Security State*. Minneapolis: University of Minnesota Press, 2016.

Simmons, Debora Adams. "Why We're Devoting an Entire Issue of National Geographic to Race." *National Geographic*, 2018. https://www.nationalgeographic.com/magazine/2018/04/race-issue-examination-understanding-background/

Singh, Anneliese A. *The Queer and Transgender Resilience Workbook: Skills for Navigating Sexual Orientation and Gender Expression*. Oakland, CA: New Harbinger Publications, Inc., 2018.

Skinner, Allison L., Andrew N. Meltzoff, and Kristina R. Olson. "'Catching' Social Bias." *Psychological Science* 28, no. 2 (2017).

Steele, Claude. *Whistling Vivaldi: How Stereotypes Affect Us and What We Can Do*. New York: W.W. Norton, 2010.

Steptoe, John, and John Stevens. *Mufaro's Beautiful Daughters: an African Tale*. New York: Amistad, 2019.

Stevenson, Robin. *Pride: Celebrating Diversity & Community*. Toronto: CNIB, 2016.

Sue, Derald Wing. "How Unintentional But Insidious Bias Can Be the Most Harmful." Interview by Judy Woodruff. PBS NewsHour, November 13, 2015. https://www.pbs.org/newshour/show/how-unintentional-but-insidious-bias-can-be-the-most-harmful.

———. *Microaggressions in Everyday Life: Race, Gender and Sexual Orientation*. Hoboken, NJ: John Wiley & Sons, 2010.

Swenson, Hayley. "What Is the Future of Paid Parental Leave in America?" *Pacific Standard,* April 2, 2019, https://psmag.com/social-justice/the-future-of-paid-parental-leave-in-america.

Tatum, Beverly. "Talking about Race, Learning about Racism: The Application of Racial Identity Development Theory in the Classroom." *Harvard Educational Review* 62, no. 1 (1992).

———. *Why Are All the Black Kids Sitting Together in the Cafeteria?: And Other Conversations about Race*. New York: Basic Books, 2017.

Taylor, Mildred D. *Rolling Thunder, Hear My Cry*. New York: Puffin Books, 2016.

Teachers Pay Teachers: Teaching Resources & Lesson Plans. Teachers Pay Teachers. Accessed December 30, 2019. http://www.teacherspayteachers.com/.

Teich, Nicholas. *Transgender 101: A Simple Guide to a Complex Issue*. New York: Columbia University Press, 2012.

Texas Health Data. Texas Department of State Health Services. Accessed December 23, 2019. http://healthdata.dshs.texas.gov/VitalStatistics/Birth.

"The 1619 Project." *The New York Times*, August 14, 2019. https://www.nytimes.com/interactive/2019/08/14/magazine/1619-america-slavery.html.

Thomas, Angie. *The Hate u Give*. London: Walker Books, 2018.

————. *On the Come Up*. New York: Balzer Bray, 2019.

Trent, Maria, Danielle G. Dooley, and Jacqueline Dougé. "The Impact of Racism on Child and Adolescent Health," *Pediatrics*, 144, no. 2 (August 2019). https://pediatrics. aappublications.org/content/144/2/e20191765.

Villarosa, Linda. "Medical Inequality," in "The 1619 Project." *The New York Times*, August 14, 2019.

Watson, Renée. *Piecing Me Together*. New York: Bloomsbury, 2017.

Whittington, Hillary. *Raising Ryland Our Story of Parenting a Transgender Child With No Strings Attached*. Turtleback Books, 2016.

Williams, Dana. *Beyond the Golden Rule A Parent's Guide to Preventing and Responding to Prejudice*. Montgomery, AL: Teaching Tolerance, 2013.

Williams, Thomas Chatterton. *Self-Portrait in Black and White: Unlearning Race*. New York: W.W. Norton, 2019.

Woodson, Jacqueline. *Harbor Me*. New York: Nancy Paulsen Books, 2018.

Woodson, Jacqueline, and López Rafael. *The Day You Begin*. Toronto: CNIB, 2019.

Yang, Gene Luen, and Lark Pien. *American Born Chinese*. New York: First Second, 2006.